MILLER'S

COLLECTING
the 19**70**s

KATHERINE HIGGINS

contents

introd

As a youngster who grew up in the 1970s, I count myself lucky. It was the decade when things seemed to take off faster then ever before, especially with the birth of home electronics. I remember the day I was given my first pocket calculator – rudimentary by today's standards but a leap into the future as far as I was concerned. It was equally thrilling when I unwrapped my first digital watch: hardly slimline or discreet but state of the art nonetheless.

Memories of watching the marriage of Princess Anne in 1973 on the new colour television still come flooding back. Apart from the pomp and circumstance of the big occasion, it remains etched on my memory thanks to the thick shag-pile carpet on which the television sat. It seems like only yesterday that my parents' bathroom was festooned in floral wallpaper, breakfast was served on busy Kathie Winkle china, and I coveted my neighbour's Chopper bicycle. Those were the days when I was proud to be seen in brown corduroy flares, a sequinned boob tube and a Punk T-shirt littered with safety pins. But what goes around comes around, and after a lengthy gap the 1970s are now hip again.

Researching and writing this book has been a shock: I'm astounded by how many of my family and friends have kept 1970s goodies. Recounting the joys of fondues drove one old schoolmate to delve into her attic and dust down a long-forgotten boxed cooking set. My mother

uction

and sister-in-law were equally enthusiastic, producing all manner of things I had assumed lost. One colleague unveiled a cluster of halterneck dresses that she'd secreted for years, while another in the United States remembered she'd kept her Nixon campaign badge. The real shock came when I revealed the value of these items today!

The retro look of the 21st century draws much of its style from the groovy 1970s. As you flick through the first section of this book you'll notice how much our modern living environment is influenced by the designs of the decade. Carpet-hugging furniture, functional oven-to-tableware, textured glasses and vibrant fabrics all seem as much at home now as they were then. The second section traces the 1970s look through fashion: "medallion man" swaggering in polyester shirts, and 1970s women blurring the lines of dressing with bell-bottomed trouser suits. We complete this unique guide with a look at a run of unforgettable playthings, from Stylophones to Kojak boardgames, classic movie posters for blockbusters like *Jaws* and *Star Wars*, and first editions from celebrated authors such as Alex Haley and Stephen King.

It only remains for me to thank everyone who helped make this book possible. Countless dealers, collectors, colleagues and family members have given up precious time and imparted knowledge. It is only through their key mementoes and memories that the 1970s have come alive.

The highpoint of the Queen's Silver Jubilee celebrations took place in June 1977. A formal procession through London was preceded by the lighting of a giant bonfire in Windsor Park and of beacons across the United Kingdom. Waddingtons made a series of jigsaw puzzles to commemorate the Jubilee – this one depicts postage stamps from around the world bearing the Queen's portrait and those of other members of the royal family.

£15–25/$25–45

1970 1971

chronology

- Germaine Greer's *The Female Eunuch* is published.
- Troops from the United States are sent to Cambodia to attack Communist bases.
- Charles de Gaulle dies.
- Simon & Garfunkel top the charts with *Bridge Over Troubled Water*.
- Boeing's 747, the world's first jumbo jet, enters commercial service.
- IBM's floppy disk is launched.
- The Conservatives, led by Edward Heath, gain power in the United Kingdom.
- The hit film *Love Story* stars Ryan O'Neal and Ali MacGraw.
- The Equal Pay Act comes into force in Britain.
- Football World Cup – England loses to Brazil.
- First New York Marathon is run around Central Park.
- The Beatles split up as they record their last songs at the Abbey Road studios.

- Walt Disney World opens in Florida.
- Andrew Lloyd Webber's hit musical *Jesus Christ Superstar* opens in London's West End.
- Greenpeace opposes nuclear testing by the United States off the coast of Alaska.
- Britain changes over to decimal currency.
- Glam-rockers T Rex, Slade and Mud reign supreme in pop charts.
- Open University programmes begin on British radio and television.
- Voyager I and II space probes are launched.
- Hot pants come into fashion.
- Cigarette advertising is banned from American television and radio.
- *Ms* magazine is launched.
- Don McLean releases the album *American Pie*.
- Idi Amin and rebels topple the government in Uganda and seize power.

For British telephone users the Trimphone was a blessing. Packed with "novel features" like dial illumination, tone calling and a "unique handset", it was the very latest in design style. £45–55/$80–95

"Decimalization will align the structure of our monetary units with the structure of the language we talk," proclaimed the Earl of Halsbury from the Decimal Currency Board. When the time came for Britain to change over in 1971 a currency converter like this was invaluable. £5–6/$9–11

1972 1973 1974

- President Nixon and Mao Tse-tung hold historic talks for world peace in China.
- Teenybop idol Donny Osmond records his hit *Puppy Love*.
- Philips markets first home video recorder.
- Strategic Arms Limitation Talks (SALT 1) are held between President Nixon and Leonid Brezhnev to curb the nuclear arms race.
- The Tutankhamun Exhibition at the British Museum draws two million visitors.
- *Cosmopolitan* magazine is launched in Britain on the crest of the wave of women's liberation.
- Liquid-crystal-display (LCD) watches become the ultimate in timepieces.
- *The Godfather*, *Cabaret* and *Last Tango in Paris* highlight the year in movies.
- Eleven Israeli team members are murdered at the Munich Olympic Games.
- The Nike company is founded, spawning a craze in running shoes.
- The Duke of Windsor dies in exile in France.

- A 70 per cent increase in oil prices leads to a 3-day week in Britain.
- NASA launches Skylab space station.
- The United Kingdom joins the EEC along with Denmark, Norway and Ireland.
- Princess Anne marries Captain Mark Phillips.
- Queen Elizabeth II opens the Sydney Opera House.
- London's Stock Exchange allows women on the trading floor.
- Pablo Picasso, the artist, dies at age 91.
- Value Added Tax (VAT) is introduced in the United Kingdom.
- The look for men includes moustaches, bellbottom trousers, wide ties, polka dots and prints.
- Roger Moore becomes the new James Bond in *Live and Let Die*.
- Bic invents the disposable lighter.
- The California-based company Marin invents the mountain bike.
- The World Trade Center skyscraper is completed.

- President Richard Nixon resigns over the Watergate scandal.
- Alexander Solzhenitsyn is expelled from the Soviet Union.
- *People* magazine débuts, launching the era of celebrity journalism.
- The first McDonald's restaurant opens in London.
- Labour comes to power in the United Kingdom under Harold Wilson.
- Abba wins the Eurovision Song Contest with *Waterloo*.
- Women's libbers win the battle to have "Ms" written on their passports.
- The invention of Spandex makes lightweight body shapers possible.
- General Motors introduces the catalytic converter.
- The seventh Earl of Lucan disappears after his children's nanny is found murdered.

Musician Mike Oldfield played more than 20 instruments to perfect the sound of his epic composition Tubular Bells *of 1973. £2–3/$3–5*

Now in London's High Street Kensington, the new six-floor Biba store sold everything from wallpaper to a take-home meal, as this in-store newspaper from 1973 reveals. £18–20/$30–35

This depression-era caper won the Oscar for Best Picture in 1973. £130–150/$235–270

1975 1976 1977

- The Vietnam War ends, while the Khmer Rouge sweep to power in Cambodia.
- Microcomputers come on sale in the United States home market.
- The American Apollo and Soviet Union Soyuz 19 spacecraft dock.
- T-shirts, bellbottom trousers and platform shoes are the height of cool.
- The X-ray body scanner is developed.
- The Queen Mother celebrates her 75th birthday.
- The Queen opens the first pipeline to bring oil from the North Sea.
- IBM introduces laser printers.
- The Sex Discrimination Act is passed.
- Bill Gates develops the prototype of the world's first PC. As a result, he forms Microsoft.
- The Bee Gees' *Jive Talkin'* leads the disco trend.
- Egypt re-opens the Suez Canal after eight years.

- The Chinese leader Mao Tse-tung dies.
- The Romanian gymnast Nadia Comaneci scores a run of perfect tens at the Montreal Olympics.
- Concorde comes into service with British Airways for the first time.
- British Rail introduces high-speed trains reaching speeds of 143 mph.
- Pierre Trudeau is elected prime minister of Canada.
- J. Paul Getty, oil tycoon, dies.
- *The Muppet Show* begins on television.
- *Roots*, written by Alex Haley, narrates a life of slavery.
- America celebrates its bicentennial.
- Viking I lands on Mars and sends back the first close-up pictures.
- Wonder Woman is hailed as a feminist superheroine.
- James Callaghan replaces Harold Wilson as the United Kingdom's prime minister.
- *The Good News Bible*, a pioneering modern translation, is published.

- The film *Star Wars* breaks all records, winning seven Academy Awards.
- The disco craze spreads worldwide with John Travolta's smash-hit movie *Saturday Night Fever*.
- Red Rum is the first horse to win the Grand National for the third time.
- The rock 'n' roll singer Elvis Aaron Presley dies in Memphis.
- The Pompidou Centre for the Arts is opened in Paris.
- Queen Elizabeth II's Silver Jubilee celebrations include street parties and bonfires.
- The first mass-produced personal computer – the Apple II – is launched.
- Over one million skateboards are sold in the United Kingdom.
- The Sex Pistols release their controversial single *God Save the Queen*.
- Sir Freddie Laker launches Skytrain – cut-price air travel.

"The classic Executive Memory: precise, powerful and elegant." In 1973 this Sinclair calculator was billed as "the slimmest, lightest, best-looking calculator in the world". £160–180/$290–325

"You've got to ask yourself one question, do I feel lucky. Well, do ya, punk?" In The Enforcer *(1976) we see another classic* Dirty Harry *performance from the gritty American actor Clint Eastwood. £300–400/$540–720*

1977 was a memorable year for the United Kingdom as the Queen celebrated her Silver Jubilee. This dish is just one of the thousands of commemoratives. £8–10/$15–18

1978 1979

- Britain's first test-tube baby is born.

- Pope John Paul II elected – the first non-Italian pope for 400 years.

- The supertanker *Amoco Cadiz* spills oil on the Brittany coastline.

- John Travolta co-stars with Olivia Newton-John in the popular nostalgic 1950s film *Grease*.

- Konica introduces the first point-to-shoot autofocus camera.

- Golda Meir, Israeli political leader, dies.

- Coca-Cola signs a deal to have exclusive selling rights in China.

- *Superman*, the movie starring Christopher Reeve, opens.

- Madhur Jaffrey presents the first British television series on Indian cookery.

- Philips markets the Laserdisc.

- Tory leader Margaret Thatcher becomes the United Kingdom's first female prime minister.

- An atomic leak at Three Mile Island, USA, almost causes a nuclear disaster.

- Sebastian Coe becomes the first athlete in the United Kingdom to hold three world indoor records simultaneously.

- Pineapple Dance studio is founded by Debbie Moore.

- Lord Mountbatten is killed by an IRA bomb.

- The Prestel computer information service is launched.

- John Wayne, actor, dies.

- Sony launches the Walkman radio.

- Ayatollah Khomeini stages coup in Iran.

- Mother Teresa receives the Nobel peace prize for her work with the world's poor.

- The Soviet Union invades Afghanistan.

- The first spreadsheet program, called "Visicalc", is released.

- The sci-fi horror movie *Alien* is released.

- Egypt's President Sadat and Israel's Prime Minister Begin sign a peace agreement at the White House.

- *Evita*, the musical, opens on Broadway.

Grease was a feel-good 1950s-revival film that grossed more than $360 million worldwide, making it the most successful musical movie of all time. £8–10/$15–18

Elvis Costello used a picture of Sinclair's new "tiny tele", the MTV1 (see p.45), on his second album, entitled This Year's Model *(1978). £3–4/$5–7*

The arrival of
the disco decade signalled all-
change in the home. It was goodbye to space-
age 1960s interiors and hello to the rustic textures of
hessian cladding, which mixed comfortably with wood pan-
elling, cork tiles and shag-pile carpets. Convenient wipe-down
vinyl wallpapers proved perfect for a splash of colour and all-over pattern. "Suddenly everyone was looking over their shoulders to the
Twenties and Thirties for inspiration," recalls British fashion designer
Jeff Banks. "Brown and cream were the order of the day," he adds, and
the Bohemian look was all about mixing old style with new. As more
homes embraced open-planning, fashionable low-slung furniture
was tailor-made to fit snugly into corners. Gadget manufacturers pulled out the stops to free housewives, but
some accessories were so time-consuming
to clean that they defeated their objective. But
for women who enjoyed the lifestyle presented by
Nova *magazine in 1973 this was hardly a concern* –
they lived with an emerging breed, the house husband,
"who exchanged bread-winning for bread-making".

homestyle

italian seating

Italian designers set the pace for 1970s homestyle: bean-bag chairs by Zanotta or low Dralon-covered lounge seats were key features of any living-room. International shows like "Italy: The New Domestic Landscape; Achievements and Problems of Italian Design", staged in New York (1972), put the new-wave Italian look under the spotlight. Two camps existed, the Modernists who put function and rationalism first, and the radical Anti-Modernists, who were more conceptual and alternative, mocking élitism in design in an attempt to popularize it. Italian designers received great acclaim for their innovative use of plastic for seating, but when the Oil Crisis hit in 1973, such democratizing ideas were turned on their head. Cutting-edge seating appeared in small runs, and these limited-edition rarities are much prized today.

← Designer Joe Colombo (1930–71) always knew how to give furniture a contemporary twist. To ensure a modern feel for this Birillo bar stool, designed for the Milanese firm Zanotta c.1970, he combined leather-look vinyl with a chromed tubular-steel frame and a fibreglass base, which ingeniously concealed four castors. This could have appeared clumsy, but Colombo achieved a flow from top to toe. Because his career was tragically cut short by his death in 1971, originals like this are much sought after.

£800–1,000 | $1,400–1,800

← This Libro (book) chair was an innovative response from the collective Gruppo D.A.M. (Designers Associati Milan) to the need for versatile furniture to fit in with multi-purpose living spaces. "Skim through an armchair and sit on a page," said advertising from manufacturers Busnelli in *Domus* magazine, presenting it as the ultimate in adjustable seating – the vinyl-coated "leaves" flip over to convert the Libro from formal upright chair to laid-back recliner. Its leather-look upholstery worked well in 1970s rooms in which the doors were fashionably padded.

£1,000–1,500 | $1,800–2,700

→ This Michael Thonet chair of 1978 set new ground rules. Working for Studio Alchimia, Alessandro Mendini (b.1931) proved that original ideas were alive and kicking by giving classic objects a modern makeover. He took an acknowledged masterpiece of the Victorian era by Michael Thonet (1796–1871) and added his own outrageous extras. Attached to the back of the bentwood frame was a palette of colour with balls firing in every direction – a mass-produced chair had become a spectacle, ensuring that Mendini got his redesign point across.

| £1,100–1,300 | $2,000–2,350 |

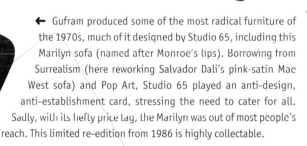

"skim through an armchair and sit on a page"

← Gufram produced some of the most radical furniture of the 1970s, much of it designed by Studio 65, including this Marilyn sofa (named after Monroe's lips). Borrowing from Surrealism (here reworking Salvador Dali's pink-satin Mae West sofa) and Pop Art, Studio 65 played an anti-design, anti-establishment card, stressing the need to cater for all. Sadly, with its hefty price tag, the Marilyn was out of most people's reach. This limited re-edition from 1986 is highly collectable.

| £2,500–3,500 | $4,500–6,300 |

→ A classic but far from classical, the Attica seat was designed by the radical collective Studio 65 for Gufram. The column segment (which you would expect to see outside the Parthenon rather than inside your living-room!) was made from moulded polyurethane foam. Studio 65 dispensed with the Modernist notion of truth to materials – the only thing the Attica was capable of supporting was the person who sat in it. For real impact, it could be accompanied by a matching column table.

| Table and chair set | £3,000–5,000 | $5,400–9,000 |

→ This boxing-glove chair of 1978 from the Swiss design company DeSede was its idea of a modern-day chaise-longue. The company was famous for its spirited use of leather in the 1970s. Those who lounged on the boxing glove had something in common with Rolls-Royce and Bentley owners – DeSede provided sumptuous leather for their cars' interiors. The fact that you probably had to own a luxury car to be able to afford cutting-edge design like this did not seem to hamper sales. The chair is still made today, but surprisingly few originals are around, making those that exist seriously prized.

£1,500–2,500 $2,700–4,500

"the perfect modern foil for a less than interesting Baroque armchair"

← Proust's Armchair was another piece of seating from Alessandro Mendini (b.1931) that embodied the redesign ideals of Studio Alchimia. In 1976 Mendini had undertaken a fabric commission for Cassina which had been inspired by the French novelist Marcel Proust (1871–1922), a firm admirer of Impressionism. Two years later Mendini played on it by taking a detail from one of Paul Signac's Pointillist works. Blown up, it is the perfect modern foil for a less than interesting Baroque armchair. Those who saw it first time round were forced to think hard about what Mendini believed was the banality of 1970s mass-designed objects.

£7,500–8,500 $13,500–15,300

← Consumerism boomed in the 1970s, and an even wider choice of mass-market products was available. Billboards, coupon offers, catchy radio jingles and television advertisements reinforced branding. In his 1962 painting *200 Campbell's Soup Cans*, Andy Warhol stripped away the advertising hype to reveal the truth about how similar every-day mass-produced items really are. The painting obviously inspired this "Omaggio ad Andy Warhol" stool from 1973. Gavina, the Bologna-based firm which made it, was paying homage to Pop Art values, indicating that designer furniture should not be élitist. The stool was made from a recycled paint drum, screenprinted with Campbell's classic soup label.

| £350–450 | $630–810 |

→ Strawberries and cream, tea on the lawn and roses are typically English, middle-class and conventional, all of which infuriated the Italian designers Giorgio Ceretti, Piero Derossi and Ricardo Rosso. Together they combined to under-mine preconceived "good taste" and play around with quaint English values by creating this Wimbledon lounge chair for Gufram in 1974. The square seat is covered with a synthetic grass fabric, and a detachable cushion upholstered in floral chintz was added. For flexibility the chromed steel legs unscrew.

| £2,500–3,500 | $4,500–6,300 |

← Although this Sedilsasso (stone seat) appears to be rough and solid like a boulder, the moulded polyurethane structure is actually flexible and smooth. Designed by the radical Piero Gilardi (b.1942) for Gufram, the Sedil-Sasso follows on from his smaller I Sassi (rock) seat. Both pieces challenged conventional ideas about furniture style and were a real talking point at the "Eurodomus 3" exhibition in Milan (1970). The weather-resistant lacquered coating made them ideal inside or out.

| £400–600 | $720–1,100 |

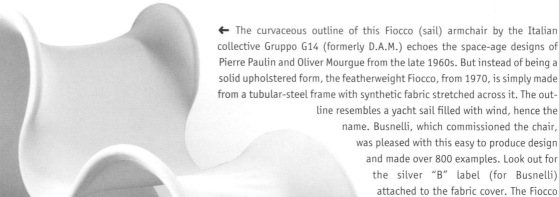

← The curvaceous outline of this Fiocco (sail) armchair by the Italian collective Gruppo G14 (formerly D.A.M.) echoes the space-age designs of Pierre Paulin and Oliver Mourgue from the late 1960s. But instead of being a solid upholstered form, the featherweight Fiocco, from 1970, is simply made from a tubular-steel frame with synthetic fabric stretched across it. The outline resembles a yacht sail filled with wind, hence the name. Busnelli, which commissioned the chair, was pleased with this easy to produce design and made over 800 examples. Look out for the silver "B" label (for Busnelli) attached to the fabric cover. The Fiocco has a permanent place in the Museum of Modern Art, New York, which significantly enhances its collectability.

| £1,500–2,000 | $2,700–3,600 |

→ La Cova (nest or den) was an early 1970s avant-garde design that blurred the lines between what was seen outdoors and in. Its designer, Gianni Ruffi, borrowed from nature, and styled his seat in the shape of a bird's nest. Instead of twigs, La Cova was made from overlapping woollen scraps, stitched together. It was scaled-up to provide discreet seating for two. Castors on the base meant that La Cova was a truly flexible piece of furniture. This example is from the first production run, 1973–74.

| £4,000–6,000 | $7,200–10,800 |

← Marion Baruch's Ron-Ron is covered in furry fabric, has a long tail, and appears more like an animal than a chair. For the manufacturers, Gavina, the Ron-Ron was perfect for their Surrealist-inspired Ultramobile collection. "Today, we, who live in an era ... dominated by functionality, rationality and methodology, must inevitably expect to generate controversy with Ultramobile", said Dino Gavina (b.1932). Other pieces included an "eye" chair (Le Temoin) designed by Man Ray, and an apple-filled upturned bowler hat (MAgriTTA), inspired by René Magritte's paintings. All are sought after today.

| £600–900 | $1,100–1,600 |

← This Synthesis 45 typist's chair by Ettore Sottsass Jnr (b.1917) was designed to integrate with a series of modular office units (System 45) that he created for Olivetti. Today its vibrant canary-yellow base hardly seems radical at all, but in a conventional 1970s work environment where black and grey dominated it would have turned heads. Sottsass had worked with Olivetti since the 1950s, and this was another of his clever designs – the frame swivelled, the seat was adjustable and the back dropped down if a stool was required. As technology rapidly progressed and the size of office equipment was substantially reduced, furniture for the office was under pressure to keep up. Units from the System 45 modular range quickly became out of date; however Sottsass's typist's chair lived on.

| £400–600 | $720–1,100 |

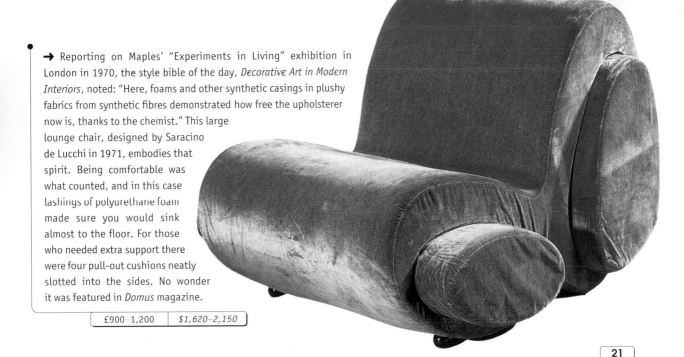

"... in a conventional 1970s work environment where black and grey dominated it would have turned heads."

→ Reporting on Maples' "Experiments in Living" exhibition in London in 1970, the style bible of the day, *Decorative Art in Modern Interiors*, noted: "Here, foams and other synthetic casings in plushy fabrics from synthetic fibres demonstrated how free the upholsterer now is, thanks to the chemist." This large lounge chair, designed by Saracino de Lucchi in 1971, embodies that spirit. Being comfortable was what counted, and in this case lashings of polyurethane foam made sure you would sink almost to the floor. For those who needed extra support there were four pull-out cushions neatly slotted into the sides. No wonder it was featured in *Domus* magazine.

| £900–1,200 | $1,620–2,150 |

→ This is wild seating quite literally! Named Pratone (meaning meadow), this seat, exhibited in 1972, was the culmination of Italy's most eccentric design ideas, and came from the radical Gruppo Sturm. The big blades of foam grass brought nature right into living-rooms. For real impact, it was suggested that units were linked together, but with each measuring over 1m wide, a lot of space was needed, and this may be why so few were bought. Charles Stendig, founder of the firm that distributed the Pratone in the United States, suggested that as few as two in as many years were sold there. Apart from the rare originals, look out for limited-production reissues, which are also favourites with collectors.

| £3,500–5,500 | $5,250–8,250 |

"wild seating quite literally!"

← Alessandro Mendini's (b.1931) Kandissi sofa from 1979 represented the radical opinions of Italy's Anti-Modernist designers. Mendini, who broadcast his ideas through his furniture and the influential design magazines he edited – *Casabella* and later *Domus* – was determined to break down élitism. In this case he mocked the belief that art was superior to design, taking a 19th-century sofa as his model but giving it his signature twist with applied geometric panels. The vivid colours and asymmetrical shapes are a direct reference to the Russian-born artist Wassily Kandinsky, the father of modern Abstract painting.

| £9,000–13,000 | $13,500–19,500 |

↑ Kitchen design in the 1970s was all about open-plan style, provided that there was a "road block" serving centre to divide the preparation and dining areas. Stools like these played a key role, and, as *Good Housekeeping*'s *Encyclopaedia* from 1971 pointed out, "they can be a great comfort for the many jobs that can be done more restfully sitting down". The Italian designer Anna Castelli Ferrieri (b.1920) designed this run of varied height stools for Kartell in 1979. When not being used they could usefully be tucked under the counter top or kitchen table. Each incorporated key features that *Good Housekeeping* claimed were vital: a firm stance, a backrest "to add comfort", and "a washable finish".

| £300–500 | $540–900 | Each

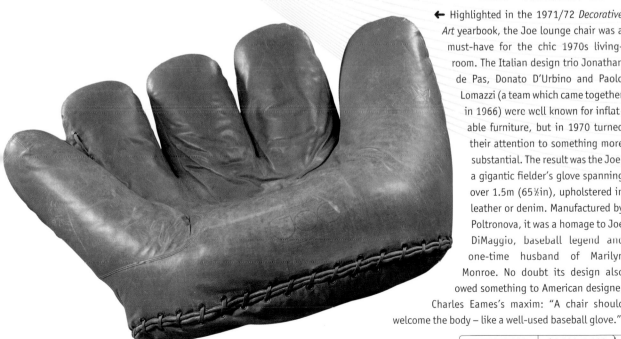

← Highlighted in the 1971/72 *Decorative Art* yearbook, the Joe lounge chair was a must-have for the chic 1970s living-room. The Italian design trio Jonathan de Pas, Donato D'Urbino and Paolo Lomazzi (a team which came together in 1966) were well known for inflatable furniture, but in 1970 turned their attention to something more substantial. The result was the Joe, a gigantic fielder's glove spanning over 1.5m (65½in), upholstered in leather or denim. Manufactured by Poltronova, it was a homage to Joe DiMaggio, baseball legend and one-time husband of Marilyn Monroe. No doubt its design also owed something to American designer Charles Eames's maxim: "A chair should welcome the body – like a well-used baseball glove."

| £2,500–2,800 | $4,500–5,000 |

international seating

Around the world, furniture designers were adapting to changing lifestyles. In 1970 the Ciba Foundation stressed that "a house should be a general purpose shell ... capable of adapting to any needs ...". Much of the response which was unveiled at the Stockholm and Copenhagen Furniture Fairs (1970 and 1971) revolved around portable designs. As talk of flexibility in design spread, so did the quantity of low-level spongy modular furniture, which provided a Bohemian relaxed feel. Materials became the challenge of the decade. In the United States cutting-edge modern also stood for Craft Revival and increased reliance on natural materials such as wood and cane. Frank Gehry found that the synthesis between humans and their furniture came from humble corrugated cardboard, while the Japanese designer Shiro Kuramata tamed sheets of industrial glass for his living-room seating.

← This aptly titled Homme chair must have provided a focal point in any fashionable 1970s living-room. Ruth Francken (b.1924), the designer, opted for a sculptural approach, while her contemporaries concentrated on translating the human form into sinuous upholstered seating. In 1971, 20 black or white Homme chairs were issued. This white version, made from moulded fibreglass and resin, dates from 1985, when a further limited run of the series was produced.

| £5,000–6,000 | $9,000–10,800 |

↓ In the 1960s, furniture by the Finnish designer Eero Aarnio (b.1932) featured in the cult British television series *The Prisoner* (first shown in 1967) and the sci-fi film *Barbarella* (1968) to reinforce the notion of futurism. A decade later Aarnio was still a master of futuristic design, although looking to materials other than moulded plastic and fibreglass. This velour upholstered Pony chair is a scaled-up version of a child's toy. It graced the boardrooms of American corporate giants, presumably to enliven business meetings. But outside the contract market, retailers Stendig sold few examples, so you will not find many around today.

| £5,000–6,000 | $9,000–10,800 |

→ This modular seating system from 1971, designed by the German Burkhard Vogdherr (b.1942) for Rosenthal, was ideal if you weren't sure how many guests you would be entertaining at your fondue party. It epitomized the multi-purpose line that ran through modern homestyle in the 1970s. The graduated seating sections, covered in fashionable shades of brown fabric, could be arranged in any number of ways to fit into the space that was available. Clip-on plastic utensil trays with drop-in ashtrays were a convenient extra for snacks, cutlery and the obligatory cigarette.

| £3,000–4,000 | $5,400–7,200 |

"clip-on plastic utensil trays"

← The Swedish designer Jan Ekselius (b.1946) incorporated all the latest technology and materials in his Etcetera seating. Hidden within the upholstery is a complex support system of steel springing and elastic, softened by a covering of foam and washable velour. Public spaces, advertising agencies and architects' offices were all homes for Ekselius's enterprising design. In Sweden the furniture firm JOC manufactured it until 1979; in the USA it was distributed by Stendig. It is reproduced today in limited numbers by Swedish-based Etcetera Design – proof of its enduring style.

| £450–550 | $810–1,000 |

◄ From the man who gave us the first commercially successful single-form plastic chair came this System 1-2-3 chair in 1973. Its Danish designer, Verner Panton (1926–98), relied on the cantilever principle to craft this wildly contoured outline, which was suitable for both boardroom and living-room. It was a truly versatile piece of design, easily adaptable to suit its purpose with the factory addition of armrests, castors or a swivel base. Upholstery varied, from buttoned suede and patterned velvet to brightly coloured fabric like this.

Castor armchair £300–350 | $540–630
Swivel armchair £300–400 | $540–720

➔ It's as if the Danish designer Verner Panton had a premonition of the impending Oil Crisis and its effect on the plastics industry when he came up with this chromed-steel and wire curvaceous seating system for the manufacturer Fritz Hansen in 1971. It was a move away from the single-form plastic chairs that had brought him so much acclaim in the 1960s. Describing his approach Panton said: "I try to forget existing examples ... and concern myself, above all, with the material. The result then rarely has four legs, not because I do not wish to make such a chair, but because the processing of materials like wire ... calls for new shapes."

£3,000–4,000 | $5,400–7,200

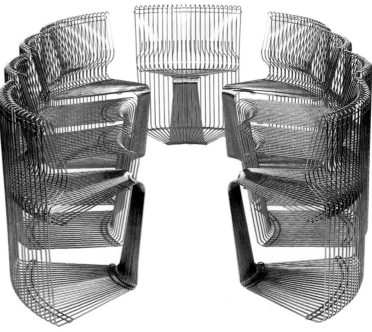

"... they were making beauty"

↑ Low-slung chrome-and-leather chairs were part of the relaxed 1970s lifestyle. The interiors bible *Decorative Art* for 1972/73 waxed lyrical about their so-called "knock down" construction that put those who sat in them a few inches from the floor. These were made by the Norwegian firm Westnofa Furniture. The condition of the leather is important – anything too worn or cracked is not worth considering unless it is associated with a key designer.

Each	£130–200	$235–360

→ The Canadian Frank Gehry (b.1929) was drawn to corrugated cardboard because artist friends "were working with ... broken wood and paper, and they were making beauty". His Easy Edges series included 17 pieces, among them this lounge chair and "wiggle" stool (1972). US-based Jack Brogan made originals like these for just three months. In 1982 they were reissued by Chiru; today Vitra Editions reproduces selected models.

Chair	£3,000–5,000	$5,400–9,000
Stool	£4,000–4,500	$7,200–8,100

← This Sunball chair was the ultimate in flexible design. Its German creators, Günther Ferdinand Ris and Herbert Selldorf, created more than just a simple seat for the manufacturers, Rosenthal Einrichtung. It was a weather-proof lounge chair for one or two, where you could eat (courtesy of pull-out side trays), sleep (the seat tilted almost flat) or just relax and listen to music (thanks to integral Blaupunkt hi-fi and speakers). For an extra bit of privacy the lid could be locked, and a built-in lamp provided appropriate mood lighting.

£6,600–8,000 | $11,900–14,400

→ "Seating that fits snugly into the corners of a room makes the most of space," advised *Ideal Home* magazine in 1971. This angular lounge suite made by the Finnish furniture firm Asko met all the new furnishing demands. Both the three-seater sofa and the armchair could be drawn right up against the walls, which helped to keep the living environment fashionably open plan. Although the tomato-red upholstery looks astonishingly vivid to us today, it was in hot demand throughout the 1970s, as magazines like *Homes & Gardens* proved with their interior features titled "The Glowing Impact of Red".

£400–500 | $720–900

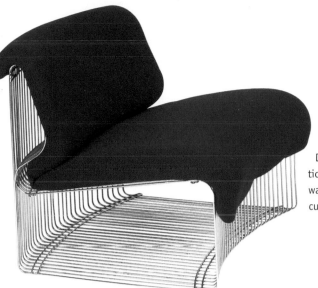

← Wire-framed seating was a popular way of reducing the bulky look of living-room furniture. This Pantonova waiting chair from 1971 shows how hard designers like the Dane Verner Panton (1926–98) worked to transform traditional solid upholstery into something more open. The result was a relaxing lounge chair which allowed light and air to circulate, and which appeared to hover above the floor.

| £300–400 | $540–720 |

→ Three-piece suites were passé for fashionable interiors. To be modern, according to *Ideal Home*, you had to "furnish with flexible change-around furniture". So what could be better than a chair that you could see straight through, which did not obscure the room? The Japanese designer Shiro Kuramata (1934–91) came up with this clean-cut solution in 1976, replacing the blow-up plastic seating of the 1960s with industrial float glass. Only 40 were made, and, with many in museum collections, examples are cherished and valuable.

| £10,000–12,000 | $18,000–21,600 |

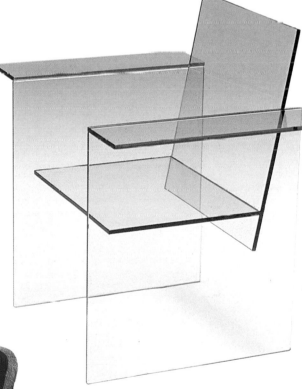

"Three-piece suites were passé"

british seating

Britain was a hotbed of creativity in the 1970s, and this was widely recognized abroad. Designers such as the influential Geoffrey Harcourt were commissioned by overseas firms to find new styling solutions that would bring them face to face with an international market. Success resulted from a run of softly upholstered stand-alone pieces. Manufacturers moved away from the ubiquitous three-piece suite, and they were backed up by interiors magazines. "Consider buying a sofa as a piece of furniture in its own right," said *Ideal Home* in 1971. And the place to see what was on offer was the newly opened British Crafts Centre in London. As the decade progressed so did British seating. "In the furniture industry there is a marked return to natural materials," noted *Decorative Art in Modern Interiors*. "The varied, subtle textures of wood are replacing the gloss of plastics," it observed in 1978. Britain was at the forefront of the 1970s craft revival, thanks to the furniture maker John Makepiece. His school in Dorset gave its students an unrivalled grounding in a range of furniture-making techniques.

↑ Truly relaxing, the Cleopatra (or 248) sofa paid homage, in many ways, to the sculptured lines of late-1960s pieces by Pierre Paulin. It also marked a move forwards for its Dutch manufacturer, Artifort. Keen to broaden the international appeal of its furniture, it turned to the British designer Geoffrey Harcourt (b.1935). His Cleopatra sofa was so distinctive that it regularly popped up in contemporary movies. The same is true today of modern editions, manufactured by Sitag under licence from Artifort.

| £1,000–1,200 | $1,800–2,150 |

← Anthropomorphic seating, as exemplified by this Elephant lounge chair from the designer Fred Scott (1942–2001), broke with the traditional formality that had dominated living-rooms since the arrival of the three-piece suite way back in the 1920s. With sculptural stand-alone seating like this, modern 1970s homestyle was taken in an altogether more relaxed direction. The Elephant chair was designed for the British furniture firm Hille in 1972.

| £1,200–1,500 | $2,150–2,700 |

→ Fred Baier (b.1949) was one of a new generation of British designers who questioned the status quo. When he exploded onto the scene with original designs like this, it was clear that function played second fiddle to craftsmanship. Of primary importance for Baier was how the chair was put together, not how much support it offered the person seated. It was a novel notion, conceived in the 1970s but firmly explored by Baier and his followers in the 1980s. Picked out as a leading light by the Crafts Council for its 30-year retrospective exhibition (held in 2000), Baier is an acknowledged master whose early work is appreciating in value.

| £1,000–1,500 | $1,800–2,700 |

← This chair in turned and laminated sycamore was handmade by designer John Makepiece (b.1939), a key force in the craft revival movement that swept through Britain and the United States in the late 1970s. "Hand-craftsmanship", he said, "is a sort of fiesta of the object: it transforms the everyday utensil into a sign of participation." The finest quality was what counted, and he championed the use of the best woods. Look out for the John Makepiece Workshop mark on the underside of the seat.

| £1,600–2,000 | $2,900–3,600 |

→ The original version of this Fesse (buttock) seat of 1970 by the British-born Roy Adzak (1927–87) was made from plaster. After completing his design he famously said: "Good art is not what it looks like, but what it does to us." Adzak was trying to achieve something that not only looked original but was also very comfortable. It was only after his death in 1991 that 25 copies were produced in France by Atelier A. This limited-run reproduction was made from GRP plastic but still retained its comfortable feel.

| £1,300–1,500 | $2,350–2,700 |

tables and desks

"It's surprising how useful occasional tables are," said *Ideal Home* magazine in 1971. Like much homestyle in the 1970s they were conveniently multifunctional: a low table could double as a seat or a magazine rack, depending on your requirements. Glossy white plastic and painted-wood finishes predominated, as did smoked glass. However, there was a revival of traditional materials for dining-tables, and wood began to take the place of plastic, which had spiralled in cost as a consequence of the Oil Crisis. At this time the dining-table had various roles to play. One was as a showcase for the new rustic-look oven-to-tableware, which fitted in with the trend for self-sufficiency and vegetarianism. Another, according to *Good Housekeeping's Home Encyclopaedia*, was as "a study or writing desk". Tailor-made desks were often reworkings of traditional designs. And while plastic was still affordable, in the early 1970s, many Italian designers took this opportunity to explore all-in-one moulded-plastic designs, many of which had built-in pen and paper compartments.

↓ The combination of shiny white surfaces and smoked glass summed up much of 1970s homestyle. Plastic was an obvious way to achieve "the look", but some firms, as in this case, opted for plywood that could be painted. Occasional tables like this became the mainstay of many living-rooms – the lower the better, to suit the decade's ground-hugging sofas and chairs. Here it serves as a stand for a reading lamp, but in other homes it could be used as a television table. When you are buying painted furniture like this, watch out for chips and scratches. It can be difficult to identify period examples, and the fact that a designer or manufacturer cannot be attributed to this piece reduces its value.

£100–150 | *$180–270*

← This vibrant red state-of-the-art Oryx desk is a good example of functional design – the combined efforts of two Italians, V. Parigi and Nani Prina, in 1970. Just like a traditional school desk it has a lid, only this time in glass. The classic inkwell has been replaced with a series of built-in compartments for stationery, and a flip-up lamp meant that users could see what they were doing. The Oryx was available at upbeat design shows like the "Salon de Mobili" in Milan (1971), along with a matching chair. Look out for the manufacturer's label on the underside; it reads "Molteni & Co, Italy".

£1,200–1,400 | *$2,150–2,500*

➜ This pine dining-table, by the Italian Enzo Mari (b.1932) for Simon International, marked a move away from the reliance on plastic that had dominated cutting-edge furniture in the early 1970s. Mari took a highly sculptural direction when using wood. The base was inspired by 1920s Russian Constructivist architecture. Nothing was hidden, and you could see exactly how the table was put together, suggesting that it was far from élitist.

£3,500–5,500 | $6,300–9,900

← This Oozo 700 mini desk proved a favourite with young visitors to Italy's popular furniture fair, the "Salon de Mobile", in Milan in 1971. French designer Marc Berthier (b.1935) successfully turned mouldable GRP (glass-reinforced polyester) into a bench-cum-desk that was perfect for any youngster. This innovative design included a shallow well for pencils and crayons and a deep hollow for books and toys – details that would have been expensive to produce in other materials.

£250–350 | $450–630

"a bench-cum-desk ... perfect for any youngster"

➜ As well as designing office equipment in conjunction with Olivetti, the Italian designer Ettore Sottsass Jnr (b.1917) also turned his hand to office furniture. The relatively simple lines of this desk, designed for Poltronova in 1970, made it easy to mass-produce. However, changes in office planning and reductions in equipment size meant that its giant 5½ft (1.8m) span did not fit in a decade later. Needless to say, it is rare to find a survivor like this today.

£1,200–1,500 | $2,150–2,700

← For those who did not want to be tied down to the way their furniture looked there was the Colonnato table designed by the Italian Mario Bellini (b.1935) for Cassina in 1977. Truly versatile, its lacquered marble top came with the option of being supported by three, four or, as seen here, five columns, to be arranged as you wished. But the sheer combined weight of top and base (1,320lb/599kg in the case of the largest in the series) precluded too much indecision. Bellini won the Resources Council of Design Award for this design in 1978.

| £1,000–1,700 | $1,800–3,000 |

→ The British designer Alan Peters (b.1933) received many commissions for his highly individual work that linked the traditional qualities of wood with industrial materials such as aluminium, which could be shaped using woodworking tools. These dual-material designs fitted in with the 1970s boom in central heating. "I had to allow timber to move freely," says Peters, who still designs today, so small details like the inset aluminium stringing in the walnut top served both a decorative and a functional purpose. After 1975 his furniture was influenced by a trip to Japan, and is characterized by the use of end-grain.

| £300–500 | $540–900 |

← Despite being supremely stylish and surprisingly comfortable, this Boccio dining set by the Italian firm Ipi was never going to be a mass-market seller, primarily because it was made from plastic and launched just before the Oil Crisis in 1972. So the well-thought-out organic lines and easy-to-stack interlocking chairs went to waste because few were made or sold, hence its collectability today. Each piece is clearly marked with a label detailing designer, model and maker.

| Set | £800–1,000 | $1,450–1,800 |

→ In the 1950s the established French sculptor Philippe Hiquily (b.1925) gained a name for himself with his static mobiles that were welded from metal. It is no surprise to see him using the same welded-steel construction for this table-base some 20 years on. Just like his sculptures, the look was delicate but strong – essential considering the weight of the smoked-glass tabletop above.

| £2,500–3,000 | $4,500–5,400 |

← This Harlow occasional table conveyed the same look as the Harlow dining-suite, both the work of Ettore Sottsass Jnr (b.1917) for the manufacturers Poltronova. For this low-lying table, a scaled-down elliptical platter of smoked glass tops the classic aluminium pedestal. Bringing a material like aluminium into the home paved the way for the high-tech look that dominated design in the late 1970s and 1980s. Gurus of the decade consider the resulting look to be truly 1970s and will pay handsomely for it.

| £1,000–1,500 | $1,800–2,700 |

35

storage

In 1972, the main type of housing in France and West Germany was the apartment, which did not often provide the luxury of spare space. Similarly, new towns in Britain and cluster-home developments in America promoted a more compact living environment. Faced with shrinking homes, 1970s designers were forced to find solutions to the age-old problem of storage. Much of what emerged was flexible – cocktail units doubled as magazine racks, plug-together shelving expanded with your reading habits, and storage units housed both your cutlery and your hi-fi system. There was an all-pervading sense of compactness, with its champion being the gifted Italian Joe Colombo. Sadly his untimely death in 1971 left many of his ideas to be explored by others in this decade. One such designer was Ettore Sottsass Jnr, who turned multi-purpose furniture into modular storage units. Flexible mass-housing needed storage that was supremely versatile, and Sottsass designed the ultimate solution with a component living system that was unveiled in 1972.

→ Here are two examples of 1970s reworkings of the humble coat stand. The Italian designers Guido Drocco and Franco Mello took homestyle into a completely new direction with their painted-foam Cactus coat stand. Close up it is very realistic, and cleverly blurs the lines between what is man-made and what is natural. Gufram produced few originals, but a limited run of 2,000 was re-issued in 1986. If the Cactus was just a little too quirky then there was always Sergio Asti's slimline coat-cum-umbrella stand from the mid-1970s. Its gleaming chromium-plated steel shows how a growing number of designers were bringing industrial materials into the home.

Left	£2,000–2,700	$3,600–4,850
Right	£180–220	$325–395

← The Boby trolley made from versatile glossy ABS plastic was unveiled in 1970 by Joe Colombo (1930–71). For additional storage you could remove the pen tray and clip on more sections. To distinguish Colombo's design from others, check for his signature on the bottom shelf. Bieffeplast, its original manufacturers, recently licensed the Italian firm B-Line to produce the Boby today.

£250–350	$450–630

→ Keeping household "apparatus" to a minimum was one of designer Joe Colombo's (1930–71) dreams. The easy-to-clean plastic laminate body of this aptly named LivingCentre Service Unit had a built-in cutlery tray and lots of storage behind a protective roll-down shutter. There were compartments for a pull-out bin and a hi-fi system, with room for speakers in specially cut grilles. When shown at the 1972 "New Domestic Landscape" exhibition in New York it was attached to a Daybed and Dinner Element, complete with hotplate and refrigerator. The Oil Crisis later made this type of furniture expensive to produce.

£2,000 3,000	$3,600 5,400

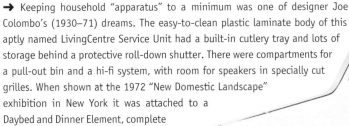

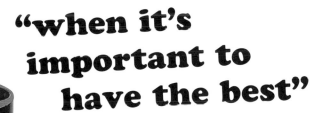

"when it's important to have the best"

← These two slick plastic designs would have complemented most early 1970s interiors. The yellow floor ashtray by the Italian firm Brevattato, with its classic "push to open" mechanism, kept unsightly cigarette ends hidden. Designers responded to information about the harmful effects of tobacco on health by disguising smoking accessories like this as stand-alone pieces of furniture. The slogan used to advertise this Pluvium umbrella stand in *Domus* magazine (November 1971) summed it up perfectly: "When it's important to have the best." Designed by the Italian Giancarlo Piretti (b.1940) for the makers Anonima Castelli, with its innovative swivel discs it eliminated the old problem of wet and dry umbrellas mixing. Today it is regarded as a classic, and collectors are keen to find pristine examples.

Ashtray	£45–55	$80–95
Umbrella stand	£180–200	$325–360

← Cheese-and-wine parties were key to sophisticated 1970s entertaining. And what better way of making sure that drinks were on hand than with this cocktail unit? Made for the Italian firm Astarte, it typifies the decade's style with its shiny white fibreglass shell and smoked-glass shelf. A deep central compartment stored bottles while other low-lying shelves provided space for glasses. Lifestyle magazines showed how the unit could look good even after the party, filled with a few pot plants.

£250–350 | $450–630

→ Open-plan 1970s living was all very well, but it needed a tidy mind to stop clutter spoiling the look. On hand were stylish sets of storage drawers like these by the Italian designer Simon Fussel. They were launched by Kartell in 1974, the year that *Homes & Gardens* magazine ran a feature on the most popular tint of the day: "Colour it Red" said the headline. Swivel castors doubled the drawers' usefulness.

£300–350 | $540–630

← Truly modular furniture was the aim of many designers. This unit by Ettore Sottsass Jnr (b.1917) was one of a series of prototypes displayed at the Museum of Modern Art's "Italy: The New Domestic Landscape" show in New York (1972). The idea revolved around a core "module" (with inner and outer frames) which could be expanded by linking it to others. Here the wardrobe section in the foreground is joined to two other modules that provide cooking facilities. But Sottsass's versatile solution remained "a series of ideas and not a series of products", so this is a rare and treasured item.

£6,000–10,000 | $10,800–18,000

↑ The Italian trio that had brought the world the first mass-produced inflatable chair, the Blow chair, in 1967, turned their hands to something altogether more substantial this decade. In keeping with the huge contemporary demand for modular furniture, Jonathan de Pas, Paolo Lomazzi and Donato D'Urbino used solid plastic bricks for these shelving units for Longato, which could be arranged to suit the particular needs of the individual.

| £2,000–3,000 | $3,600–5,400 |

"Open-plan 1970s living was all very well ..."

← How convenient to have a cupboard that you could wheel to wherever you wanted it. This was exactly what the Italian design guru Giovanni (Gio) Ponti (1891–1979) achieved with his Apta Series Compactum, which was conveniently portable, and ideal for any space in the home or office. Nothing less innovative was expected from Ponti. After all, he was the architect and designer who had styled Milan's Pirelli Tower of 1956, and he had also founded and edited the influential design magazine *Domus* as long ago as 1928.

| £1,500–2,000 | $2,700–3,600 |

lighting

"Lighting is part of decoration, every bit as essential as wallpaper or paint," said *Ideal Home* magazine in 1971, adding: "It is one of the less expensive ways of improving the appearance of a room, cheap to run and nowadays easy to install." Advances in technology during this decade enabled designers to be much freer with their solutions. Shortly before his death in 1971, Joe Colombo championed the use of a single halogen lamp to light the whole room. Fibre optics, track lighting and low-voltage bulbs were all incorporated into new-look ceiling, floor and table lamps. The accent was on flexibility and variable lighting, and at every home's heart was the ubiquitous dimmer switch. Such innovations helped break down the barriers between indoors and outdoors. This was spurred on further by improvements in garden lighting. While some designers came up with "finger-tip control" and touch-sensitive lights, others focused on adjustable lighting that spotlit a room's special features. The overriding tendency, reflected the Italian designer Achille Castiglioni, was to emphasize "the decorative quality of fixtures when they are without light".

← The architect-turned-designer Vico Magistretti (b.1920) linked up with Knoll to produce this Colleoni lamp – a new take on traditional street lighting, with delicate smoked-glass spheres that seemingly might float away. The expensive murano glass shades on this example point to a early production piece – they are inscribed "Colleoni Lamp / K / 1971 Venice". In 1977 Magistretti adapted the lamp for O-Luce and it is still in production today.

£1,000–1,500 | $1,500–2,250

→ Apart from the innovative seating that brought him worldwide acclaim, the Danish designer Verner Panton (1926–98) created equally impressive lighting during the 1970s. Panton's most well-known piece is this Panthella lamp, mainly because modern editions, still made by the lighting giant Louis Poulsen, sell so well today. Although the mushroom-shaped shade was widely copied, no imitation could match up to Panton's original with its innovative multi-switch, which could be pressed once for a 50 watt light, a second time for 100 watts, a third time for 160 watts, and a fourth time to turn off the lamp. Watch out for the rarer chrome version.

£400–500 | $600–750

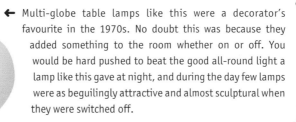

← Multi-globe table lamps like this were a decorator's favourite in the 1970s. No doubt this was because they added something to the room whether on or off. You would be hard pushed to beat the good all-round light a lamp like this gave at night, and during the day few lamps were as beguilingly attractive and almost sculptural when they were switched off.

| £500–600 | $900–1,100 |

"few lamps were as beguilingly attractive"

→ Perspex, a type of acrylic plastic, was a favourite material in the 1970s as homeware, lamps included, became more sculptural. The fact that it was easily moulded and crystal clear meant it lent itself to abstract geometric styling. *Domus* magazine advertised similar designs to this, which towered upwards from the floor or table, almost in honour of great 1970s architecture, such as London's high-rise Barbican centre designed by Chamberlin, Powell & Bon. There are no clues as to who made this lamp, but its style is a give-away of the period.

| Pair | £700–750 | $1,250–1,350 |

← The idea of a giant snail lurking in the corner of your living-room was never going to have wide appeal, but the Italian designer Sergio Cammilli (b.1920) believed it would have its supporters. Made by Bieffeplast in 1974, the naturalistically moulded fibreglass shell offered more than quirky looks: it was a clever way of bringing the outside in. It was a light aimed at home-improvers – devotees of extensions with patio doors who longed, as *Ideal Home* said, for "fingertip access to the garden".

| £1,500–2,000 | $2,700–3,600 |

→ "Special features, or furniture, can be enhanced by special lighting," noted *Ideal Home* magazine in 1971. And what better way to achieve pinpoint lighting than with this vibrant Hikary light designed by Ettore Sottsass Jnr (b.1917) for Skipper in 1976. An integral square bracket meant that the skeletal Hikary could be suspended from the ceiling with the lamp section hanging below it from four wire cables. To fit in with a variety of modern interiors, the Hikary came in a range of colours from the yellow you see here to bright tomato red.

| £600–800 | $1,100–1,450 |

"slick design and sheer size"

← In highlighting the craze for fibre-optic lamps, the style magazine *Nova* was mesmerized by the "pinpricks of light at the end of each glass fibre". Experiments using glass fibres for communications took place in the 1960s, but in 1970 scientists working for Corning Glass manufactured hair-thin pure-glass fibres capable of carrying 65,000 times more information than copper wire. Almost as swiftly as they were scooped up by industry, glass fibres appeared in lamps for the home. Price tags were hefty – this cost £97 in 1970 (over £500 or $750 today) – but declined as the decade progressed. Watch out for 1980s revivals with plastic instead of glass fibres.

| £50–80 | $90–145 |

→ Contemporary photographs show just how dramatic this Mefistole ceiling light looked against the backdrop of a pure white ultra-modern 1970s interior. The brainchild of Ettore Sottsass Jnr (b.1917) for Stilnovo, this was a light that stood out in its own right mainly as a result of its slick design and sheer size – top to toe it measured over a yard (one metre). Like a stalactite the chromed-metal shaft hung down from the ceiling. The fact that taller visitors would have needed to walk around it just added to its presence. Look out for the maker's name, Stilnovo, stamped on the metal ceiling bracket.

| £500–700 | $900–1,250 | *Each*

← This intriguingly spiky lamp called Sinvola da Tavolo was designed by the Italian Michele de Lucci (b.1951). It was hardly run-of-the-mill with its bold use of colour and alternative design materials such as hat-pins. But de Lucci intended it to make a dramatic statement as soon as you walked into the room. Conceived at a time when a number of Italian designers, of whom de Lucci was one, wanted to break away from Modernist design, it took a highly radical conceptual stance. Many design museums have been snapping up key 1970s pieces like this for some time – if you too can live with this, then now is the right time to buy.

| £1,500–1,600 | $2,700–2,900 |

"a distinctively icy feel"

→ There is a sense of Japanese capsule-living about this lamp base with one cube built upon another. It also matches much of the Nordic-style glassware that was being produced in the early 1970s in the way it conveys a distinctively icy feel with its moulded-glass sections. Without a maker's mark to indicate its exact origins it remains a slight mystery, but it is typical of the decade. Clear glass was a popular material for lamp bases in the 1970s because its translucency accentuated rather than distracted from open-plan living spaces. At night, with a lamp shining down through the glass sections, it would have created a spectacular lighting effect.

| £265–285 | $475–510 |

technology

The 1970s saw an explosion in electronics innovation. It came largely at the expense of European manufacturers, whose dominance was rapidly worn away by Japanese electronics giants. At first they were accused of design plagiarism before proving to be truly ahead of the game with the launch of groundbreaking gadgets such as the Sony Walkman in 1979. At the forefront of change was the world's first microprocessor, the legendary 4004, launched by America's Intel Corporation in 1971. Many could hardly believe that a chip the size of a thumbnail was as powerful as the world's first electronic computer, ENIAC (1946), which had filled an entire room. As less expensive, more powerful chips followed, so did electronic gadgets. Hewlett Packard and Sinclair were months apart with their pocket-sized scientific calculators in 1972. The same year Philips unveiled the first true video-cassette recorder with a tag of around £300 (£1,650 or $2475 today). Some companies, such as Olivetti, turned to designing slick cases for their products. Other companies, such as Apple, were more concerned with what was inside the box. The two elements came together in some of the new hi-fi equipment.

← If you didn't own a calculator at the beginning of the decade you were certain to have one by its end. In 1972 Hewlett Packard introduced the first pocket-sized calculator, the HP35, priced at $395. Hot on its heels in the same year came the 2⅛oz (56g) Sinclair Executive, at £79.95, from the electronics genius Clive Sinclair. He remained firmly wedded to LED (light-emitting diode) displays, as is shown by the Oxford Universal (1975). Others, such as the Japanese Casio Computer Company Ltd with its FX-2000 (1975), correctly identified that LCD (liquid-crystal display) would become the standard. Calculators like these, even the humble Prinztronic M, made in Hong Kong for the UK Dixon's Group in 1975, are hot collectables today.

Prinztronic M	£8–10	$15–18
Sinclair Oxford Universal	£40–60	$75–110
Casio FX-2000	£15–20	$25–35
Sinclair Executive (boxed)	£160+	$290+

← Plastic was key to television design during the 1970s. In a highly competitive market, moulded-plastic cases in fashionable "decorator colours" beat veneered and painted wooden rivals hands down – even though they were never as well made. The Japanese electronics firm JVC unveiled this new upbeat design, the Videosphere television, in 1970. Its space-helmet shape, complete with a smoked acrylic "visor" in front of the screen, was clearly influenced by the success of the Apollo mission to the moon in 1969. Watch out for the other colours available too, with grey being one of the most sought after.

£200–300 | $360–540

→ The Trimphone (model 712 telephone) was probably the most widely mimicked piece of technology in this decade (see p.10). On the Continent, this telephone by the Swiss makers Trub mixed all the tradition of wood with the modernity of push buttons, giving just about as much cachet as you could want in the 1970s! The varied wood finishes were designed to synthesize with stylish panelled interiors, which were very much in vogue this decade. Its angular outline, reminiscent of a computer keyboard, was another reminder of the modern age.

£85–90 | $155–165

← Clive Sinclair and his firm Sinclair Radionics Ltd were determined to innovate in the field of television too. At its launch, in 1977, Silver Jubilee year, this MTV1 (microvision pocket television) was the smallest pocket television for all standards on sale. "Tiny Tele!" raved the headlines, "different from anything else in the world." It measured a mere 6 x 4 x 1½in (15 x 10 x 4cm) with a 2in (5cm) screen, and in 1978 it won a prestigious Design Council Award. All you needed to make it work were the built-in rechargeable batteries.

Boxed | £100+ | $180+

→ At its launch in 1976 this Zoom SLR (single-lens reflex) camera from Minolta was the first ever made for 110 film. Taking advantage of the popularity of inexpensive colour 110 cartridges, Minolta promised that this camera would achieve a result to rival conventional 35mm SLR cameras – only the bonus here was that Minolta's version was half the weight and was, like 110 Instamatics, very compact. However, it was also expensive, unlike either its cousins or its film, and, despite the flexibility of the fixed zoom lens over basic 110 models, the processed quality never really matched that of the larger format film.

£30–50	$55–90

← Thanks to transistor amplifiers, cabinet-sized radiograms were being replaced by more compact hi-fi (high-fidelity) systems. Improved stereo quality plus the wider availability of stereo records made modern systems more appealing. Top manufacturers used innovative styling to set their equipment apart. Brionvega brought in Mario Bellini (b.1935) to design its Totem Hi-Fi (1971), which took the form of a discreet white cube. The speakers could be swung out, or detached and distanced for a better stereo effect. Bellini also turned his hand to Yamaha's Natural Sound stereo cassette deck (1975), neatly arranging the controls on a wedge-shaped body.

Yamaha	£200–300	$360–540

Totem	£3,000–5,000	$5,400–9,000

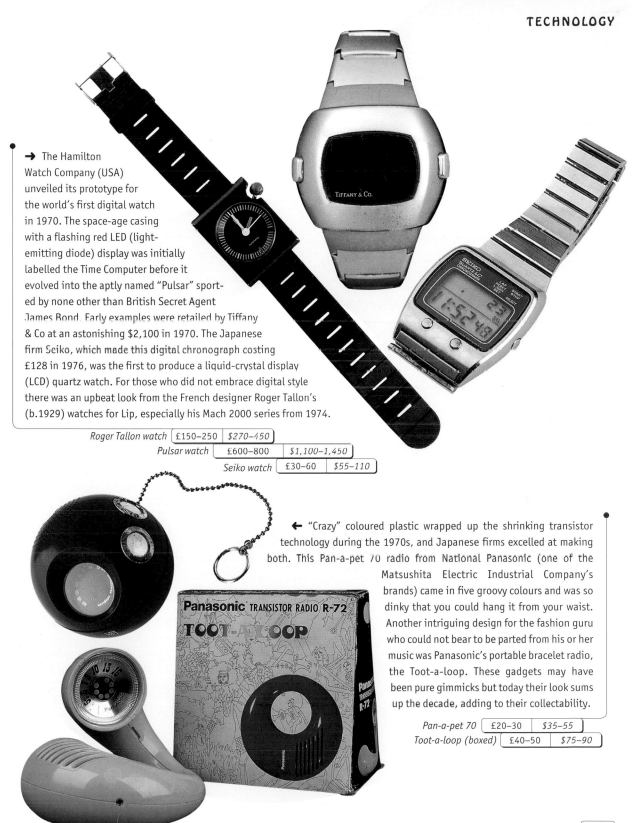

→ The Hamilton Watch Company (USA) unveiled its prototype for the world's first digital watch in 1970. The space-age casing with a flashing red LED (light-emitting diode) display was initially labelled the Time Computer before it evolved into the aptly named "Pulsar" sported by none other than British Secret Agent James Bond. Early examples were retailed by Tiffany & Co at an astonishing $2,100 in 1970. The Japanese firm Seiko, which made this digital chronograph costing £128 in 1976, was the first to produce a liquid-crystal display (LCD) quartz watch. For those who did not embrace digital style there was an upbeat look from the French designer Roger Tallon's (b.1929) watches for Lip, especially his Mach 2000 series from 1974.

Roger Tallon watch	£150–250	$270–450
Pulsar watch	£600–800	$1,100–1,450
Seiko watch	£30–60	$55–110

← "Crazy" coloured plastic wrapped up the shrinking transistor technology during the 1970s, and Japanese firms excelled at making both. This Pan-a-pet 70 radio from National Panasonic (one of the Matsushita Electric Industrial Company's brands) came in five groovy colours and was so dinky that you could hang it from your waist. Another intriguing design for the fashion guru who could not bear to be parted from his or her music was Panasonic's portable bracelet radio, the Toot-a-loop. These gadgets may have been pure gimmicks but today their look sums up the decade, adding to their collectability.

Pan-a-pet 70	£20–30	$35–55
Toot-a-loop (boxed)	£40–50	$75–90

→ The Walkman spawned a haircut, entered our dictionaries as a noun, found a permanent spot in museums worldwide and revolutionized the way in which people listened to music. What more can be said of Sony's Walkman, model TPS-L2 – the world's first personal stereo? Fortunately for all of us, Akio Morita, co-founder of the Sony Corporation, went against the advice of colleagues who failed to recognize the demand for a cassette player that did not record. At its launch in July 1979 it was a marker of things to come. Within two months of the initial production run, 30,000 units had been sold, and a pocket-sized music revolution was well on its way.

£30–60 $55–110

← While others pinpointed size as an issue, Olivetti focused on ergonomics, and the sheer pleasure it afforded users, for its Divisumma 18 calculator (1973). Alluringly tactile, its keys were sealed under a thin rubber skin that undulated like the craters on the moon. Contemporary space talk may or may not have provided inspiration for its Italian designer, Mario Bellini (b.1935), but the humble desk calculator was now an attractive as well as a functional piece of equipment. Condition helps to attract a collector's eye.

£50–100 $90–180

← With hand-held video cameras still a decade away, the 1970s family was content to relive the holiday with a slide show or Super 8mm film. The Japanese giant Canon stole a march on competitors with its Cine Canonet 8, a development of the popular Canonet lens shutter arrangement of the 1960s. Super 8 technology already existed but took off this decade as users realised that you only had to pop a sealed cartridge into a camera and shoot. After Kodak unveiled its Ektasound film in 1973, the prize for manufacturers became a cine camera capable of integrating recorded sound with footage. This Nizo Integral 5 from 1979 by the German makers Braun was one of the most advanced. Collectors admire such equipment for its slick design and are keen to snap up models with original boxes, labels and instructions.

| £100–150 | $180–270 | Canon Cine Camera (with case) |
| £100–150 | $180–270 | Nizo Integral 5 |

"it undulated like the craters of the moon"

→ From the Apple Computer company, the firm that ignited the PC revolution, came this truly innovative Apple II computer (1977). It was the first personal computer with colour graphics to be sold in a plastic case. The downside was that for a hefty $1,298, you could only type in capital letters, but it came with a colour screen and built-in sound. Compared with today's technology, the Apple II is basic, and most have been scrapped. Today it is a must-have for the growing band of computer collectors, especially with original software and manuals. With offers as high as $37,000 (c.£25,000) for a prototype Apple I, constructed in the garage of company founder Steve Jobs, the Apple II is sure to appreciate in value.

| £180–200 | $325–360 |

49

kitchenware

Open-plan kitchens were part of 1970s living, suiting "people with a nothing-to-hide approach", said *Good Housekeeping* magazine's book on kitchens in 1976. Guests came face to face with the kitchen's contents, so modular style units and integrated equipment grew in popularity along with co-ordinated decoration. Floral-printed pans, tins and tableware added to the unity of preparation and dining areas. To help "the au pair who refuses to abandon her mother tongue", said *House & Garden* magazine, there were labelled storage jars "to hold the nation's fuel; tea, coffee and sugar". A flurry of gadgets appeared, including the first domestic food processor, the mighty Magimix, which promised to liberate housewives. One favourite for working women was the much-trumpeted "crock-pot", but in reality it was just another item to be washed up. The United Kingdom joined the European Community in 1973, and scales, recipes and meas-uring jugs printed metric scales alongside imperial ones.

→ These plastic-cased Drink-Ups were relative newcomers to Pyrex's oven-to-table glassware range. They came in fashionable colours, and stood out from less expensive imported imitations because they offered a two-year guarantee. The 1970s were a key decade for Pyrex in Britain. James A. Jobling, the glass-maker which manufactured Pyrex in Britain and Europe, was taken over by the American Corning Corporation (the inventors of Pyrex in the early 20th century) which changed the firm's name to Corning Ltd. As a result the Jobling shield mark "JAJ" was dropped after 1975, giving collectors a clue to dating.

Boxed	£3–5	$5–9

← Entertaining in the 1970s was incomplete without a fondue set. "It adds to the fun for everyone to help themselves," said Myra Street in her *Mixer and Blender Cookbook* (1972). With the accent on versatility, this flame-powered piece of cookware could be used to make "delicious and easy" cheese, beef or even sickly chocolate meals. Users were advised not to "wield their forks" so as to avoid accidents, and owners learnt the hard way if they stood their sets on Formica sur-faces. Today a revived interest in 1970s style has meant that fondue sets are back in fashion. Condition is every-thing, and only those without scratches or chipped enamel count.

Set	£10–15	$18–25

← When it was launched in Britain in 1974, many said that the Magimix by the French firm Robot Coupe was ugly and would not last, but within two years it had become a cult item and opened a new chapter in household convenience. The Magimix was branded a "cuisine système" (kitchen system), with its blades, slicers, graters and whisks all revolving in the base of one bowl. Its powerful 800-watt induction motor, tough plastic bowl (made from the same polycarbonate plastic as Concorde's windows) and stainless steel Sabatier knife promised to last a lifetime. Robot Coupe realized that cooking and presentation were more important than laborious preparation. Look out for early models like this.

£30–40	$55–75

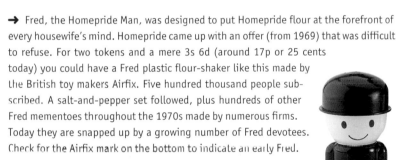

→ Fred, the Homepride Man, was designed to put Homepride flour at the forefront of every housewife's mind. Homepride came up with an offer (from 1969) that was difficult to refuse. For two tokens and a mere 3s 6d (around 17p or 25 cents today) you could have a Fred plastic flour-shaker like this made by the British toy makers Airfix. Five hundred thousand people subscribed. A salt-and-pepper set followed, plus hundreds of other Fred mementoes throughout the 1970s made by numerous firms. Today they are snapped up by a growing number of Fred devotees. Check for the Airfix mark on the bottom to indicate an early Fred.

Flour shaker	£20–75	$35–135
Salt and pepper pots	£15 60	$25–110

← "Speed up your kitchencraft," claimed the French manufacturer Moulinex. Many pieces of kitchen equipment were mechanized in the 1970s, including the carving knife. In 1971 two versions of this electric knife were available, either plug-in or cordless. Equally versatile and admired in the same year was the hand-held battery-powered whisk from the British firm Kenwood. Its designer, Kenneth Grange (b.1929), was determined to craft a gadget that people enjoyed using. Despite niggling problems, Grange's efforts led to this whisk being accepted as a design classic today.

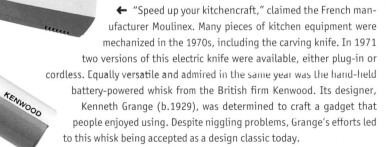

Moulinex carving knife	£5–8	$9–15
Kenwood whisk	£10–15	$18–25

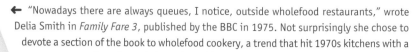

← "Nowadays there are always queues, I notice, outside wholefood restaurants," wrote Delia Smith in *Family Fare 3*, published by the BBC in 1975. Not surprisingly she chose to devote a section of the book to wholefood cookery, a trend that hit 1970s kitchens with a passion. Regarded as the British equivalent of America's popular Martha Stewart with her homely, no-fuss recipes, Smith first came under the spotlight in the 1970s with her BBC television series, also entitled *Family Fare*. Books like these that accompanied her shows are classic collectables. Ena Baxter's recipes, first published by Johnston & Bacon in 1974, spread the word about Scottish healthy eating on both sides of the Atlantic, and during the 1970s millions in the United States watched her cookery demonstrations on television.

Each	£2–3	$3–6

→ For the busy housewife who relished her independence, or the part-time worker who needed to plan ahead, the ultimate gadget was the crock-pot cooker. Fry your meat with a handful of onions, pop it into the slow cooker and leave it to cook while you were out for the day. Apart from the bonus of managing itself, the crock-pot saves energy by using "as much electricity as a lightbulb". Books like this that sum up the decade's fads are increasingly treasured.

	£2–3	$3–6

← The automatic egg boiler was never quite as useful as it seemed. *Which?* magazine reported that even if you used the boiler once a day it would take over 25 years to save the purchase price. Spurred on by the healthy-eating craze, those who aspired to be self-sufficient stopped buying yoghurt and started making it. This electric Salton yoghurt maker was considered one of the finer models, producing supermarket-quality yoghurt for a fraction of the price.

Yoghurt maker	£12–15	$20–25
Egg boiler	£4–5	$7–9

→ On 1 January 1973 the United Kingdom joined the European Community, and had to embrace a Common Market directive on metrication. Recipes and packaging were printed with metric measurements alongside the imperial, but the public were slow to learn. These stylish metric 4000 kitchen scales, the brainchild of the Italian designer Marco Zanuso (b.1916) for the French firm Terraillon, softened the blow. To help with the problem of conversion there were handy aids like the Metricook by the British makers Probus. Spin the wheels and you quickly learnt that 8oz was the same as 225g. Skyline, the British brand name of the American Prestige Company, produced a series of plastic measuring spoons to make sure you always got it right.

Terraillon scales	£40–50	$75–90
Metricook	£6–8	$11–15
Spoons	£4–5	$7–9

← "How nice when something that is a necessity also contributes to the décor," said *Homes & Gardens* of storage jars. "They will turn unsightly clutter into a focal point where stored foods are kept attractively within easy reach." This trio by John Clappison (b.1937) for Britain's Hornsea Pottery matched the popular country-kitchen feel. The Saffron pattern used from 1970 relied on a resist technique to stop the glaze sticking properly to the screen-printed decoration, which gave it a raised effect. In 1974 Hornsea opened a factory-cum-visitors' centre in Lancaster so that you could see sets like these being made.

Storage Jars	£4–5	$7–9	each
Vinaigrette	£2–3	$3–5	

tableware

"Casseroles, soufflé dishes and coasters that perfectly match your dinner service" were, said *House & Garden* magazine, fitting for a decade that embraced oven-to-tableware. Dining co-ordination coupled with convenience and easy stacking was what counted in the 1970s, and pottery firms like British-based Denby and Midwinter responded with a new array of shapes and patterns. Textured matt glazes reflected a return to rusticity, and the popular "country-style look" was intertwined with a wave of self-sufficiency and vegetarianism. Eating styles, combined with greater ownership of dishwashers, encouraged cutlery designers to craft more sculptural eating tools that could withstand high washing temperatures. For this reason stainless steel continued to be a favourite for many firms, and it was heavily promoted by British Steel which wasted no time in highlighting its "simplicity and strength". When it came to entertaining, the emphasis was on up-to-the-minute style. If you didn't have an au pair to help then a Hostess Trolley was deemed essential. It's "more than entertaining, it's a way of life" said the advertisements. For the increasing band of package holiday-makers there was even a range of china, courtesy of the British designer Kathie Winkle, that reflected the sunshine climates they had left behind.

← Package-holidaymakers who wanted a flavour of overseas back home snapped up patterns such as Seychelles, San Marino, Mexico and Palma Nova from the British pottery James Broadhurst & Sons. The abstract-cum-floral patterns by the designer Kathie Winkle (b.1932) were as warm and bright as the climates they evoked. During the 1970s Winkle's designs peaked, with over one million pieces made in 1974 alone. Although patterns were hand-painted in the 1950s and 1960s, the majority were applied and finished by machines in the 1970s. Even so, pieces like this Carousel plate are increasingly sought after. They are easily identified by the rubber-printed back-stamp, with the pottery's name and Winkle's script signature.

| £5–6 | $9–11 |

→ The La Boule dinner service for four by Helen von Boch (b.1938) was unveiled in 1971. It was a noted design triumph. Nineteen pieces fitted together, one inside the other, to form a neat ball-shaped sculpture for the sideboard. La Boule was part of the Avant Garde collection for the German ceramics firm Villeroy & Boch, but for some it was a little too avant-garde to be practical. "It's bad enough having to wash and dry the dishes after dinner without having to puzzle over how to turn them into modern sculpture!" said *Ideal Home* magazine.

| £80–120 | $145–215 |

"a noted design triumph"

→ Like her contemporaries, the Italian architect Gae Aulenti (b. 1927) was keen to find modern solutions for household objects. As well as innovative lighting, she also designed cutlery. This silver-plated canteen was at the luxury end of the market, but its all-in-one styling, with no bone or plastic covering the handle, was copied in stainless steel. With more dishwashers creeping into the kitchen this decade it was essential that cutlery could withstand the rigours of automatic washing. The link with Aulenti (known most recently for styling the Quai d'Orsay Museum in Paris) puts a premium on this set.

| £3,000–4,000 | $5,400–7,200 |

→ With four out of five women working, according to a 1978 survey reported in *Homes & Gardens* magazine, the role of woman as homemaker was rapidly eroded during the 1970s. Quick, ready meals were the way forward for families who worked, and consumption of convenience and frozen foods boomed. And what better way to serve "easy meals" than on plates like these? The frozen food giant Birds Eye advertised the fashionable oval-shaped plate as being perfect for a spread of "sizzling" beefburgers, baked beans and fried mushrooms: "Just the thing to give the family when they've all been working hard." This oval fish duo, equally suitable for serving fishfingers, was part of the Aquarius range from the British Washington Pottery.

| each | £10–15 | $18–25 |

→ After John and Sally Seymour's *Self-Sufficiency: The Science and Art of Producing and Preserving Your Own Food* and the hit BBC television series *The Good Life* appeared in the early 1970s, few could escape being touched by the healthy-living craze. The British firm W. R. Midwinter Ltd capitalized on the trend with its Stonehenge range. Roy Midwinter (1923–90), son of the firm's founder, was behind the new tableware settings that were hailed as "exciting" and "daring" at their launch in 1972. These Sun, Moon and Earth plates, with their Creation glaze, date from 1973.

Sun plate (18cm/7in)	£6–8	$11–15
Moon or Earth plate (25cm/10in)	£12–15	$20–25

← Hornsea Pottery's Concept tableware, designed by Martin Hunt and Colin Rawson, has a hint of streamlined 1930s style about it, but with modern 1970s shapes. Although it was a hugely popular line, you will not find much of it in Britain as it was largely exported to the United States and Canada. Cream was the first colour launched, swiftly followed by matt black (Image), grey and pink (Swan Lake) and the short-lived pale-blue glaze (Cirrus). Concept's sleek design earned it a Design Council Award in 1977, one reason why it is collectable today.

£10–15	$18–25	Cup and saucer
£8–10	$15–18	Sugar bowl

→ "You can build your Stonehenge set piece by piece without upsetting your bank manager," said the advertisement for Midwinter's new range. This three-pint casserole dish really did provide a financial bonus. Gone were the days when you needed one dish for the oven and another for the table. The 1970s was the decade that paid homage to oven-to-tableware ceramics. As well as being able to withstand the intensity of the oven, it was decoratively glazed for the dining-table, in this example with Midwinter's Flowersong design (from 1972) by Jessie Tait (b.1928) on the lid.

£10–15	$18–25

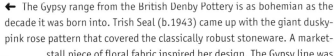

← The Gypsy range from the British Denby Pottery is as bohemian as the decade it was born into. Trish Seal (b.1943) came up with the giant dusky-pink rose pattern that covered the classically robust stoneware. A market-stall piece of floral fabric inspired her design. The Gypsy line was quick to take off from the moment it was launched in 1971 as an export range aimed at the United States. British buyers got their first taste of it a year later. The fact that it was picked out as an example of good contemporary design in *The Design Centre Tableware Buyers' Guide* (1977) added to its cachet and helped prolong its life until 1984. It is shown here with Denby's award-winning Touchstone cutlery (1974) with colour co-ordinating ceramic handles designed by Gill Pemberton and her husband Neil Harding.

Gypsy plate (25cm/10in)	£10–15	$18–25
Gypsy casserole	£25–35	$45–65
Cutlery (per piece)	£7–8	$13–15

"a more relaxed and freer style was born"

→ The cylinder was the key shape that dominated tableware in the 1960s, but as the 1970s progressed so did this fresh-look outline. The body was essentially still geometric, but, with the addition of a curvaceous handle, a more relaxed and freer style was born. These teapots from Britain's Midwinter pottery show how well the shape was suited to popular floral patterns. The prices reflect the rarity of the pattern.

Autumn teapot	£25–30	$45–55
Blue Dahlia teapot	£20–25	$35–45
Caprice teapot	£10–15	$18–25

← For the jeans and cheesecloth generation the ultimate in tea-time table-ware was Denim Ware produced by the British pottery Carlton Ware. The range, which appeared around 1978, took its lead directly from the streets where jeans were universally accepted as *the* cool-cut uniform for the young. The transfer-printed design on these pieces shows just how unisex denim fashion had become, with both genders dressed in almost identical outfits. A year after the line's release the American singer Neil Diamond cemented the denim trend with his ballad, *Forever in Blue Jeans*. But, despite great hopes for its success, Denim Ware was never a mass-market seller. Watch out for rarer items like the milk jug below.

Salt and pepper pots	£20–30	$35–55
Milk jug	£25–30	$45–55

"the ultimate in tea-time tableware"

→ The British artist David Gentleman (b.1930) beautifully captured this view of Windsor Castle for one of a series of bone-china plates issued by Wedgwood in Silver Jubilee year, 1977. With a common theme of British castles and country houses running through the images, the timing of the series could not have been better. Wedgwood jumped onto the patriotic bandwagon, knowing that its plates would be snapped up at home and abroad. Because only 5,000 of each plate were made, they are collectors' gems today.

£60–70	$110–125

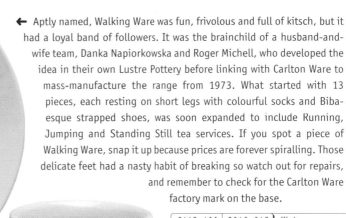

← Aptly named, Walking Ware was fun, frivolous and full of kitsch, but it had a loyal band of followers. It was the brainchild of a husband-and-wife team, Danka Napiorkowska and Roger Michell, who developed the idea in their own Lustre Pottery before linking with Carlton Ware to mass-manufacture the range from 1973. What started with 13 pieces, each resting on short legs with colourful socks and Biba-esque strapped shoes, was soon expanded to include Running, Jumping and Standing Still tea services. If you spot a piece of Walking Ware, snap it up because prices are forever spiralling. Those delicate feet had a nasty habit of breaking so watch out for repairs, and remember to check for the Carlton Ware factory mark on the base.

£115–120	$210–215	Plate
£30–45	$55–80	Sugar bowl

→ The distinctive undulating outline that bonds the pieces in this coffee set was common to a number of potteries in both the United Kingdom and Scandinavia. Here it is the work of Carlton Ware and was promoted as its Wellington shape. Records show that this set sold wholesale for £12.25, which means that it would have been an expensive purchase from new. Against a backdrop of "attractive floral" curtains, as advocated by *Homes and Gardens* magazine in 1971, Carlton's Camellia Pink pattern would have fitted in nicely.

Coffee set	£25–30	$45–55

"they're collectors' gems now"

← If you wanted tableware that was "guaranteed to make your friends' eyes pop when they drop in", raved *Ideal Home* magazine in 1971, then something by Stuart Devlin (b.1931) was a must. The Australian silversmith was classed as one of the leading designers in his field, and after a spell in the United States he settled in Britain in 1965. This limited edition set of silver beakers from 1972 marks a period of collaboration with Viners, the extinct British steel firm. The richly textured base on each beaker, highlighted in gilt, would have been a perfect match for his more numerous cutlery designs. In 2000 Devlin hit the headlines again with his series of commemorative coins designed for the Sydney Olympics.

| £1,300–1,500 | $2,350–2,700 |

"Steel Appeal in the Home"

→ In 1970 the British Steel Corporation took part in the *Daily Mail* "Ideal Home Exhibition" for the first time with its "Steel Appeal in the Home" stand. Steel was presented as a sophisticated and versatile material, with everything from a purpose-built steel kitchen to cutlery on display. Those who could afford it clamoured to own a coffee set like this. The elegant satin-finished design, styled by the British silversmith Robert Welch (1929–2000) for J. & J. Wiggin's range of Old Hall Tableware, had no name when it appeared in 1970, but a year later it was called Super Avon, with its centrepiece being "the impressive 10-cup size coffee pot". It ran until 1982 and included a now rare vacuum jug for milk. A thriving Old Hall collectors' club means that sets are always in demand.

| 3-piece set (shown) | £230–250 | $415–450 |
| Vacuum jug (not shown) | £100–110 | $180–200 |

↑ A new era in travel opened up in 1970 when the first 350-seater "jumbo" jet flew into London's Heathrow airport after its transatlantic début flight. With it came the jet-set age, and airlines which wanted to compete had to smarten up their acts for a growing number of customers. Italy's flag-carrying Alitalia Airline commissioned a fellow countryman, Joe Colombo (1930–71), to design this new in-flight tableware, all part of the airline's corporate restyling. Known for his space-saving, compact designs, Colombo did not disappoint. With its cut-off plates the Linea 72 tableware, manufactured by Richard Ginori, fitted neatly into a melamine tray and even left space for the cutlery, made by Pinti.

£700–900	$1,250–1,600	Setting for six

→ The Botanic Garden patterns by the Portmeirion Pottery revolutionized 1970s tableware. Susan Williams-Ellis, the firm's co-founder, took the designs from a 19th-century herbal book containing detailed plant and flower illustrations. The first piece, a coffee set complete with the trademark three-leaf border, appeared in 1972. Its instant appeal spawned other series, including Rose & Passionflower (1978–83) and Oranges & Lemons (1975–83). To help with dating, look at the typeface used for the names (from Latin script to modern print). In 1978 the words "dishwasher proof" and "freezer and microwave safe" appear.

Botanic Garden flower vase	£7–10	$13–18
Rose & Passionflower plate	£10–12	$18–20
Oranges & Lemons storage jar	£5–6	$9–11

ceramics

For the post-Woodstock generation the key to interior style lay with craft. Whether it was macramé, a rya rug or pottery, the emphasis was on hand-craftsmanship. Nowhere did this come together more than in the field of ceramics. This was the era of studio potters free at last to explore their own directions and receive recognition in the process. Galleries specializing in ceramics were common, and craft fairs selling the latest hand-thrown wares mushroomed. In 1971 British potters were given a boost through the newly established Crafts Advisory Committee which provided a promotional network for upbeat modern ceramic design. Even traditional pottery firms like Poole responded to changing tastes and the desire for one-offs with studio ranges of hand-decorated wares. Today, contemporary ceramics are on the agenda again, this time spearheaded by specialist auctions at major salerooms, and the spotlight is beginning to shine on 1970s studio pottery. Although it is not always possible, try to find pieces with a clear maker's seal or mark.

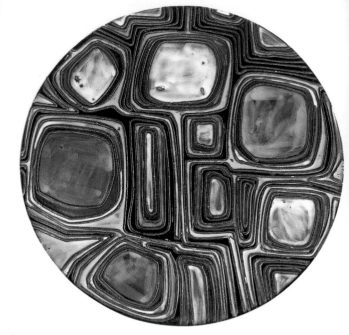

↑ "Daring and gaudy abstraction, ultra fashion of the modern beauty" was how the Poole Pottery promoted its Delphis range of hand-decorated ceramics, introduced in the 1960s. Glaze colours were rationalized around 1971, when this charger was made, and matt and semi-matt finishes replaced by a glossy look less prone to blistering. There are no initials next to the back-stamp to indicate the painter of this piece, reducing its value.

£500–600 | $900–1,100

← These shoe bookends by Carlton Ware have a Biba-esque feel about them. The English fashion designer Barbara Hulanicki (b.1936) aimed her Biba department store in London at "all optimists, fatalists and dreamers". It was a Mecca for the fashion-conscious until it shut down in 1975. The shoes on sale were not dissimilar from these, and no doubt a visit to Biba inspired some enterprising designer from the pottery. Little is known about these bookends, but they do appear in the factory's shape book and one of the pair would have carried the Carlton Ware mark.

Pair £200–220 | $360–395

→ The freedom of the studio potter came into its own during this decade as the rustic look gained a loyal following. Skilled potters like the Italian Salvatore Meli (b.1929) proudly produced pieces which showed off the fact that they had been hand-made rather than mass-produced. Glazes had a one-off experimental feel about them, a quality that added to the uniqueness of the result. This pottery charger by Meli dates from 1973.

| £2,000–3,000 | $3,600–5,400 |

← The screen-printed pattern on this plate was very much in keeping with 1970s vinyl wallpapers. It is from a series of six plates called Variations on a Geometric Theme designed around 1970 by the Scottish-born sculptor, Eduardo Paolozzi (b.1924), for Wedgwood. With a limited run of only 200 boxed sets, they were intended largely as decorative statements.

| £1,200–1,800 | $2,150–3,250 | *Set of six*

"to be viewed as stand-alone sculptures"

→ The German émigré and naturalized Briton Hans Coper (1920–81) was at the forefront of the post-war studio-pottery movement. The arrowhead shape of this Cycladic form from 1975 shows how, instead of presenting his pieces as mere vessels, Coper accentuated their ability to be viewed as stand-alone sculptures. The impact of work like this lies with its outline and size — some Cycladic forms measure well over 1ft (30cm) in height. Coper was a perfectionist, destroying anything that he felt was not up to scratch, so his work is rare and sells for a premium. Look for the prized "HC" seal on the base.

| £12,000–16,000 | $21,600–28,800 |

glass

Many great glassmaking firms were forced to fight hard to stay on top during this decade, in the face of stiff competition. Manufacturers in Eastern Europe, with their low overheads, churned out budget copies that slowly encroached on the traditional glass market. Scandinavian giants like Iittala, Orrefors and Kosta were quick to respond by exhibiting their products in stores such as Heal's in London to reinforce the quality of their wares. Promoted by the Swedish Society for Industrial Design, which celebrated its 125th anniversary in 1970, upmarket Scandinavian stores opened in Britain. One 1970s newlywed remembers: "Many of our wedding presents came from a shop that just sold Swedish glass." Talk in trade journals such as *Tableware International* was of the "textured glass" they made. Few glass firms in the United Kingdom and abroad escaped from producing glassware with surfaces crying out to be touched. Freeflowing forms emerged, counteracting the circle and the cylinder which had ruled 1960s glass design. The abstract style went hand-in-hand with the growth of the studio-glass movement in the United Kingdom and the United States. Glass artists such as Harvey Littleton (whose *A Search for Form* was published in 1971) and Samuel Herman were influential in bringing the furnace into the artist's studio so that small exclusive batches and one-off glass creations could be crafted.

→ The textured icy style of Glacier glass was about as 1970s as you could get, but had been born a decade earlier when Scandinavian glassmakers experimented with blowing into charred wooden moulds. It influenced British factories such as Whitefriars, which found a ready market for Glacier decanter and glasses sets. Cheap imitations followed and even appeared as petrol-station gifts. These carafes, which survive without their boxes, were top-end chic, designed by the Finn Tapio Wirkkala (1915–85) as part of his Ultima Thule series for Iittala. Boxed examples are prized by collectors.

Large	£32–36	$60–65
Small	£22–26	$40–45

← The Swedish Kosta glassworks, renamed Kosta Boda in 1976, received international acclaim for its art glass. Kosta's success stemmed from the award-winning artists it commissioned – among them Monica Backström, Bertil Vallien, Göran Wärff, and Ann Wärff, who designed this glass sculpture. Here Wärff counteracts the solidity of the columnar base with a band of what looks like melting icicles around the top. You are left wondering whether this is a man-made or a natural spectacle. Kosta's studio pieces are engraved with the name of the artist and the firm, the date the piece was made, and the number of editions issued.

£250–300	$450–540

← Ettore Sottsass Jnr (b.1917) was instrumental in reviving the status of Italian glass in the late 1970s, which had ridden for too long on the success of the designs produced in the 1950s. In partnership with the Murano glass factories Sottsass came up with new-wave designs like this two-tone Tazza bowl. Made by Vistossi in 1977, this is one of only 250 pieces. As a result of the limited-edition nature of many of these prestigious pieces, Sottsass's glasswares are all highly valuable collectables today.

£1,000–1,500 | $1,800–2,700

→ Samuel Herman (b.1936), the craftsman who made this vase, spearheaded the British studio-glass movement in the 1970s. His hand-blown vessels became the pride of contemporary design bibles like *Decorative Art in Modern Interiors*. Unlike mass-produced work, each of Herman's creations was individual. What you got depended on the way the coloured glass and surface flashing behaved in the studio. Needless to say, his pieces are held in museum collections around the world today. Look out for Herman's engraved script signature on the base.

£250–350 | $450–630

← The quest for new designs became a feature of the glass-making industry during this decade. At the forefront of 1970s experimentation was the British firm Whitefriars, which let loose several of its key designers to work on finding a fresh direction for their products. The resulting one-off trial pieces that they created are much prized by collectors today. This vase was the handiwork of Whitefriars' resident designer, Geoffrey Baxter (1922–95). Although a few other pieces in rich ruby-red glass are known, they cannot compare to this in size – it stands over a foot (30cm) tall! The addition of the original Whitefriars paper label makes this vase extremely desirable.

£250–350 | $450–630

→ Homeware shops selling sought-after Scandinavian designs opened all over the United Kingdom in the 1970s. The owner of these aperitif glasses recalls "spending a little bit extra on something that was good quality and looked modern". The cutting-edge Finnish firm Iittala made this duo after a design by Timo Sarpaneva (b.1926). Inspiration for much of its 1970s range came from Finland's Arctic climate, and these glasses have more than a hint of ice cube about them. The bonus is that they have survived boxed and labelled.

Pair | £20–25 | $35–45

← In addition to an engraved maker's mark on the base of this vase, the swirling blue-and-green pattern is a big clue to its origin. It was made in Malta at the Mdina Glass factory, and the skies and seas that surround the island influenced the colours. "We tried to make it indicative of Malta," says Elizabeth Harris (b.1933), wife of the late Michael Harris (1933–94), the firm's founder. Thanks to his inspired designs, Mdina Glass gained international recognition for its hand-crafted pieces. As well as the Mdina signature, this vase is particularly desirable because it carries the name of the craftsman who made it.

£120–130 | $215–235

"You couldn't live without texture in the 1970s ..."

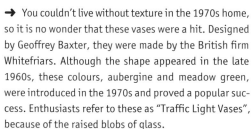

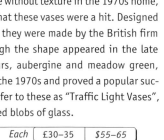

→ You couldn't live without texture in the 1970s home, so it is no wonder that these vases were a hit. Designed by Geoffrey Baxter, they were made by the British firm Whitefriars. Although the shape appeared in the late 1960s, these colours, aubergine and meadow green, were introduced in the 1970s and proved a popular success. Enthusiasts refer to these as "Traffic Light Vases", because of the raised blobs of glass.

Each | £30–35 | $55–65

← This rare glass sun disc by the British firm Whitefriars would once have hung in a Bohemian interior, but today is sought after by collectors who class it as a museum rarity. It resembles the *Bocca della verità* (mouth of truth), a giant stone mask in Rome that according to legend "will eat the hand of the one who is not sincere". Moulded in rich yellow glass, this impressive piece would have radiated a warm glow, giving the room a relaxed feel (provided that you were not the insincere type). The sunburst look had been popularized in the 1970s through a series of vases, and was achieved by using radiating strips of wire in the glass moulds.

| £95–110 | $170–200 |

→ Deep tones made the 1970s living-room "an especially warm place at the heart of things", noted *Decorative Art in Modern Interiors*, and dark colours soon filtered through to contemporary glassware. These vases hail from one of Italy's Murano glass factories. Their distinctive layered look (the *sommerso* effect) was achieved by immersing clear or coloured molten glass in a pot filled with glass of a contrasting colour. The encased gather was then either freely blown or, as here, blown into a mould to give it an angular structure. This technique was popular in the 1930s. The value of these pieces would be greater if the makers were known.

| Green vase | £50–60 | $90–110 |
| Ruby vase | £150–160 | $270–290 |

textiles

The 1970s ushered in "pattern so large that it can no longer be thought of in 'repeating' terms but as an enveloping ribbon of colour…" which "produces a cave-like atmosphere without its discomforts", according to the style yearbook *Decorative Art in Modern Interiors*. Patterns ran from muted "Biba-esque" Art Nouveau prints to pop-inspired motifs with predictably vivid colours, which eventually spawned High-Tech style. Thanks to improved screen-printing techniques and synthetic fabrics like Terylene and Bri-Nylon, most trademarked by the industrial giant ICI, the latest designs were accessible to all, and colour could be anything you wanted it to be, including "Africa brown", "Cool grey", "Cherry red" and "Warm yellow". In essence, whatever material you chose was intended to "visually enhance" your fast-shrinking living space: the wrap-around look was one clever 1970s device to fool guests into thinking a room larger than it really was through textile co-ordination. Condition is everything when collecting textiles, and however recent we may think the 1970s, many of the fabrics and carpets have suffered wear and tear. Look carefully at the selvages as they can yield important information about both manufacturer and designer.

↑ "Hot yellow and orange brings a room to life," said *Good Housekeeping* in its 1970s kitchen improvement guide. The Italian architect/designer Gaetano Pesce (b.1939) chose these tones for this Motus patterned fabric from his 1970 Expansion Collection. Versions of these overlapping squares with rounded corners, a reworking of Art Deco style, popped up frequently in 1970s interiors. Look at the selvages of fabric lengths where the designer's details are often printed.

£1,200–1,500 | $2,150–2,700 | 20m (22yd) length

↑ "Shaggy carpets, popular in America for some time, are beginning to appear in houses on this side of the Atlantic," said *Homes & Gardens* magazine in 1971. Their roots lay with the traditional Rya rugs of Scandinavia, which were used in the 14th century as bedding owing to their warmth and softness. In James Bond films during the 1970s it was more a case of relaxing by the fireside next to a token girl on one of these rugs.

£1,000–1,500 | $1,800–2,700

→ Although deeply abstract and stylized, the pattern of this screen-printed fabric is rooted in nature. Called Ikebana after the Japanese art of flower arranging, the flowing design bursts forth seeming to scatter its contents over the material like a ripe pod. Like many 1970s textile designs, it grew out of the revival of interest in naturalistic forms. The British textile designer Barbara Brown (b.1932), well known to devotees of 1970s interiors magazines, styled this fabric for Heal's Fabrics Ltd.

£75–80 | $135–145 | *per metre (39in)*

← In a decade that was in love with cork tiles and hessian wallpaper, it's no surprise that magazines like *Ideal Home* waxed lyrical about "beautiful brown". A fashionable 1970s bedroom was incomplete if it did not somehow incorporate those darkened umber tones. This easy-care Terylene (a new ICI fibre) pillow-case, part of a co-ordinating bed-linen set, was an easy and affordable way to achieve the look. At the moment it is a typical charity-shop find, but even humble items like this may soon be sought after by fabric gurus.

£2–4 | $3–7

→ The darkened interior of London's fashionable Biba department store was a look that many tried to recreate in their own homes during the 1970s. And for up-to-the-minute style, those who could afford it turned to the "designer" carpet. This one is attributed to the French fashion genius Pierre Cardin (b.1922), who was famed for his Space Age outfits in the 1960s. Its curvilinear design in deep red and purple against a black background would have set off modern furniture perfectly.

£800–1,000 | $1,450–1,800

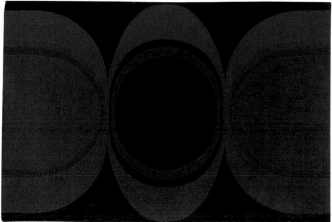

pictures and posters

With a new decade came a fresh approach to style that seemed to be summed up by eclecticism. Prints and posters were about as varied as they could be, reflecting a wide range of movements and influences. There was Andy Warhol, the Pop Art protagonist who, through such classics as his Mao portraits, brought key events and faces into the home. His interpretations were colourful and stylized, taking advantage of commercial printing methods to keep élitism at arm's length. Yet plenty of graphic artists were caught up in the wave of nostalgia that swept through 1970s fashion. And others, by incorporating designs and motifs from the past, discovered a photo-realistic style that is particularly evident in some rock-album covers of the period. Collectors snap up original prints and posters, partic-ularly those that capture the spirit of the 1970s. In the case of prints, limited editions are the most prized, while for posters, condition is the major factor in a decision to purchase.

← Op Art (optical art) pictures by the Hungarian-born artist Victor Vasarely (1908–97) were as well suited to the 1960s, when they began, as to the 1970s. By placing an array of similarly sized and shaped objects close together he managed to create a visual illusion of depth and, sometimes, movement. With interiors magazines such as *Homes & Gardens* advising their readers to make "a very definite statement with your taste … it pays to be bold", Vasarely's prints were sure to fit in. This untitled silk-screen composition dates from around 1970. Interestingly, its graphics echo what many households would soon see on their television sets when home-use video games arrived.

| £300–400 | *$540–720* |

↓ Stylized images, abstract designs and vibrant tints were essential to 1970s interiors. Thanks to the British artist Terry Frost (b.1915), one of the look's greatest exponents, rooms could have a contemporary focus. This is one of his sought-after paintings from 1971, entitled *Colour On The Side of Blue* (acrylic on canvas, 60 x 50cm/24 x 20in). Its primary colours and bold shapes were influenced by nature but pared down to a minimum. "Just to think in terms of colour is enough to set the soul alight," proclaimed Frost to a group of students. "This is colour without shape – in the spirit. Shapes are known to peo-ple by words but colour can make its own shape and exists in its own right."

| £22,000–24,000 | *$39,600–43,200* |

← Pop Art continued to march through the most fashionable interiors, and with it came the predictable explosion of colour. In 1970 *Nova* magazine showed just how good the combination of vivid plastic furniture and prints from the Pop Art master Andy Warhol (1928–87) could look when it featured the St Moritz apartment of Günther Sachs, the German millionaire playboy. Meanwhile wallpaper and clothes printed with the movement's classic images, such as Warhol's *200 Campbell's Soup Cans* (1962), continued to spread the anti-élitist, anti-high art, anti-consumerism Pop message. London's newly opened Mr Freedom shop was a natural Mecca for followers of the style. In 1974 London's Victoria & Albert Museum held a major retrospective exhibition, acknowledging the influence of the movement on current lifestyles. This poster is a rare survivor that marks the event.

£230–250 | $415–450

"the predictable explosion of colour"

→ In 1973 Barbara Hulanicki's Biba store moved to London's fashionable High Street Kensington, where there were six floors to tackle. According to *Homes & Gardens* magazine in 1974, it was the place to go for "way-out clothes and household accessories, most of which follow the 1930s idiom". The nostalgia trip was promoted by posters like this: Biba's model looks coquettishly 1930s with her bud lips and bell-hop hat surrounded by a rich array of fabrics and cushions, just the sort of merchandise Biba specialized in before closing in 1975.

£100–125 | $180–225

commemoratives

In a decade filled with political, royal, sporting and social events it is no wonder that there were so many commemoratives. The United States saw three presidents in office (Nixon, Ford and Carter), their campaigns bringing an array of memorabilia. In the United Kingdom, politics swung from left to right as prime ministers Wilson, Heath, Callaghan and Thatcher, the first woman to lead the country, held office. In 1971 the USSR leapt ahead in the Space Race, launching the world's first space station, Salyut 1, but the United States closed the gap in 1973 with Skylab. A major change for the British was decimalization, with the new currency introduced on Decimal Day, 15 February 1971. Plastic commemorative wallets of the coins were snapped up. The 1976 Bicentennial celebrations in the United States also spawned a host of mementoes. For royal watchers in 1973, all eyes were focused on the wedding of Princess Anne and Captain Mark Phillips and in 1977 on the Queen's Silver Jubilee. It is the overall quality of the commemorative items that counts. Limited-edition pieces are superior to poorly made, inexpensive equivalents.

↑ "One of the greatest games ever staged", claimed *The Sunday Times* after the first-round World Cup football match in Mexico between England, the defending champions, and Brazil in 1970. The crowd of 66,000 and the millions watching on television (the first match screened in colour in Britain) saw Brazil win 1–0, and with the help of stars Pelé and Jairzinho go on to win the coveted Jules Rimet Cup. This airline bag was one of the numerous commemoratives that marked the event.

£30–35	$55–65

← Fireworks lit up the skies and parades filled the streets on 4 July 1976, the culmination of the 200th anniversary celebrations in the United States. An estimated six million people lined the shores of the Hudson River to see a flotilla of tall ships from all over the world. President Gerald Ford opened a time capsule from the Centennial celebrations in 1876 and sealed another to be opened in 2076. Bicentennial commemoratives range from milk glasses to paper grocery bags like this rare example that is in almost mint condition. Equally unusual is the original licence plate that was available only for 1976 in the state of Pennsylvania.

£10–15	$18–25	Plate
£6–10	$11–18	Grocery bag

→ The Munich Olympic Games, held in 1972 and celebrated in this poster, are remembered as much for the record-breaking achievement of the American swimmer Mark Spitz and the captivating style of the young Soviet gymnast Olga Korbut as for the horrific murder of 11 Israeli team members. Four years later, as this plate by the British pottery Wedgwood shows, the focus of sporting talent was on Montreal. All eyes were on the gymnast Nadia Comaneci, the tiny star of the Romanian team, who scored a still unbeaten seven perfect tens.

Montreal 1976 plate	£12–15	$20–25
Munich 1972 poster	£1,000–1,500	$1,800–2,700

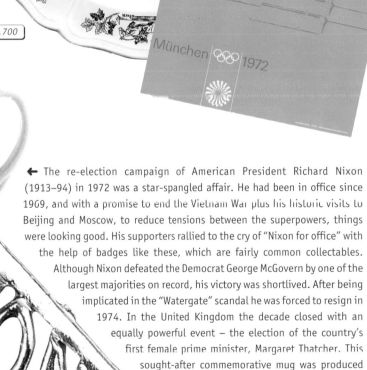

← The re-election campaign of American President Richard Nixon (1913–94) in 1972 was a star-spangled affair. He had been in office since 1969, and with a promise to end the Vietnam War plus his historic visits to Beijing and Moscow, to reduce tensions between the superpowers, things were looking good. His supporters rallied to the cry of "Nixon for office" with the help of badges like these, which are fairly common collectables. Although Nixon defeated the Democrat George McGovern by one of the largest majorities on record, his victory was shortlived. After being implicated in the "Watergate" scandal he was forced to resign in 1974. In the United Kingdom the decade closed with an equally powerful event – the election of the country's first female prime minister, Margaret Thatcher. This sought-after commemorative mug was produced to mark her landslide victory in 1979.

£14–15	$25–27	Thatcher mug
£8–10	$15–18	Nixon badges (each)

Queen Victoria's Silver Jubilee went unrecorded as it was in 1862, just a year after the death of the Prince Consort. But things were very different in 1977, and no firm was prepared to miss the opportunity – thousands of mementoes were hurried into production. *Homes & Gardens* magazine said: "You can celebrate by spending £750 on a black basalt bust or 15p on a biro." These three mugs show the diversity of what was available in one category alone. The finely printed mug on the far left was a top-quality piece made by Spode, costing £14.80 then. The mug alongside would have been far less expensive as it lacks the sophisticated gilt decoration and any trace of a maker. Carlton Ware made the novelty Walking Ware cup in front.

£45–50	$80–90	Spode mug
£8–10	$15–18	Standard mug
£45–55	$80–95	Carlton Ware cup

→ Although Queen Elizabeth II travelled a remarkable 56,000 miles (90,000 kilometres) to celebrate in an official capacity, most people remember the Silver Jubilee for informal street parties. It was an occasion to share with neighbours, so trestle tables were arranged end-to-end in suburban culs-de-sac up and down Britain. This tin of sweets from the confectioners Smith Kendon, and a bottle of Jubilee Ale brewed by Matthew Brown & Co. Ltd, are rare survivors of these celebrations. Those who watched the Queen's procession on television would have been more than familiar with the gold State Coach, dating from 1762, seen here in miniature.

Jubilee Ale	£5–6	$9–11	
Sweet tin	£5–6	$9–11	
State Coach	£20–30	$35–55	

→ Flag-waving was a preoccupation in 1977 as the Queen toured the country opening hospitals, Jubilee routes and schools. "I remember lining the route when she came to our town," said the owner of this flag. "We briefly caught a glimpse of her, which made our long wait really worthwhile." The Girl Guides Association marked the occasion by offering all its young members a small enamelled badge, shown below, and schools handed out commemoratives like the badge on the left. The owner of the transfer-printed sweet dish was given it by an aunt: "It was a national holiday and I kept it out while I watched all the proceedings on television."

Dish	£8–10	$15–18
Badges (each)	£1–2	$2–3
Flag	£3 4	$5 7

← The Queen's Christmas broadcast in 1975 took her outside the confines of her sitting-room into the grounds of Buckingham Palace, where she threw a stone into water: "Our daily actions are like those ripples, each one makes a difference …". This card from the same year, signed by both the Queen and Prince Philip, and the "thank-you" letter alongside are rarities because so little autographed material from living Royals appears on the market.

£80–100	$145–180	Christmas card
£100–150	$180–270	Letter

→ Apart from Jubilee celebrations, the other major Royal event to be marked with a host of memorabilia was the wedding of Princess Anne to Captain Mark Phillips on 14 November 1973. "All over the world 500 million television viewers looked in at the Abbey ceremony," reported *The Sunday Telegraph* in this special colour supplement that remains in pristine condition. Among the most expensive commemoratives was a pair of silver plaques etched with images of the happy couple at an astonishing £1,250 (£7,500 or $11,250 today). These wrapped matchboxes, however, originally cost only ½p each but are prized now because few exist.

Colour supplement	£4–5	$7–9
Wrapped matchboxes	£2–3	$3–5

fashion

Futuristic style may have influenced 1960s fashion but this decade's look was rooted in the past. A wave of nostalgia swept through wardrobes, championed by the doyenne of romantic dressing, Barbara Hulanicki, and her Biba department store. But despite the love of old prints and patterns, fashion's followers demanded new easy-care fabrics. Synthetics were king, and if a garment wasn't made from drip-dry Spandex, Bri-Nylon or Crimplene, it wasn't worth wearing. Later, Laura Ashley's feminine country florals printed on cotton helped to revive a fondness for natural fibres. For women, long lines ruled after the micro-mini gave way to midi and maxi lengths. Confusion over hemlines encouraged independent types, modelled on the classic "Charlie Girl", to opt for trousers. Both sexes clung to dyed blue denim throughout the 1970s, teaming their richly embroidered flares with unforgettable towering platform shoes and the ubiquitous pre-wrinkled cheesecloth shirt.

jet-set style

"Leisure clothes have arrived," trumpeted *Homes & Gardens* in 1972, adding, "it is exceedingly irritating to be labelled 'career women' after office hours." The look for the jet-set age was far less formal, and fashion took many cues from traditional ethnic outfits, which tended to be loose-fitting rather than figure-hugging. French fashion houses united with department stores over pattern: the bigger and bolder, the better. The only battleground was over the length of hemlines. "Should it be the mini or does fashion desire the midi?" was the subject of a heated British TV debate in 1970. *Nova* magazine announced the answer: the midi length was the winner, and in case you were unsure what to look for, the advice was to find dresses on which "the hem stops halfway down your leg after it has passed your knee". Women's Lib gave a further push to unisex fashions, and classic men's blue jeans became a flared fit for all. Those who yearned for a bit of femininity found solace in milkmaid-style cotton florals, the hallmark of the British designer Laura Ashley.

← The naturalism and free-flowing style of Art Nouveau design were widely embraced in the 1970s, with intertwining stems and flowers appearing on everything from casserole dishes to blouses such as this, made by the Manchester firm Crowthers. Young people were keen to find and wear vintage costume and converged on charity/thrift shops, while London's Portobello Road antiques market was doing a roaring trade in Art Nouveau treasures. Modern design did its best to imitate the old, and it is tempting to think that a nature-inspired print like this would be made from a natural fabric – but, as with many outfits in the 1970s, this one is printed onto an easy-wash man-made fibre.

| £30–50 | *$55–90* |

← Mix-and-match hemlines were a part of early 1970s dressing, and this above-the-knee dress could well have been teamed with a floor-hugging maxi coat. In the first few years of the decade anything went, and women lapped up their new-found freedom to dress as they wanted. This day dress was retailed by the smart New York store Henri Bendel. Its knitted style was ultra fashionable and echoed the sort of outfit worn by the clean-living suburban mum Carol Brady, as played by the actress Florence Henderson, in the long-running American television comedy series *The Brady Bunch* (aired 1969–74).

| £70–100 | *$125–180* |

← "Big, all-over prints, often explosive in both design and colour, are large enough to make even the most generous of figures look smaller," said *Homes & Gardens* magazine in 1971. And in their search for suitable bold motifs some designers revived ancient floral patterns. Here the French fashion house Chloë, then under the direction of Karl Lagerfeld (b.1938), mixed giant chrysanthemums with stylized peonies, two symbols often seen in historical Japanese robes. The bold look fitted well with the flowing caftan outline – a shape which suggested that even the fashion élite was attuned to the cries of the women's movement, which condemned restrictive clothing. Loose-fitting garments became a must for entertaining in the style of Margo Ledbetter, the hostess from the BBC television series *The Good Life* (*Good Neighbours* in the United States). Many, like the caftan – a Turkish man's long tunic – were based on traditional Eastern clothes.

| £100–250 | $180–450 |

→ If you stepped into London's Biba emporium in the 1970s you would find "the droopy romantic look", as *Nova* magazine described it. Those who could sew were spurred on to make less expensive look-alike outfits. The high-cut bodice of this home-sewn dress harks back to the Pre-Raphaelite era of the 19th century. The long sleeves and blouson arms were part of a flowing "damsel in distress" style. *Vogue* magazine told girls to match the dress with "porcelain pale" make-up. "Imagine you're decorating yourself for a close-up in a film of *A Midsummer Night's Dream*," they said. One housewife recalls: "We'd dress up something like this with clumpy high-heeled shoes, a beaded choker and a crocheted shawl."

| £50–60 | $90–110 |

"the droopy romantic look"

→ This maxi-dress, by the German designer Karl Lagerfeld (b.1938) for Chloë, shows how even the great Paris fashion houses were increasingly caught up in the relaxed hippie look. The streamlined style has a distinctly Japanese feel with its open sleeves, no doubt influenced by tourist souvenirs. As more people sampled less expensive air travel the real ethnic look was brought back home in suitcases filled with anything from kimonos to Turkish embroidery.

£600–700 $1,100–1,250

"leisurewear smart enough for entertaining"

← The British firm Miura gained a name for leather clothing in the 1970s. With a deft hand it elevated a material linked with a rebellious look into leisurewear smart enough for entertaining. Miura cleverly used leather as if it were fabric on these tailored long-line tops, and the co-ordinating leather strips are stitched and overlaid appliqué-style to create something that was sure to make an impact. The vivid colours and the idea of sewing leather together were things that high fashion picked up from the street style of the booming Caribbean and African communities.

Shirt	£40–50	$75–90
Sleeveless shirt	£40–50	$75–90

← For the ultimate in 1970s cool, you needed to look no further than the cheesecloth shirt. It was hip, gorgeous Agnetha from Abba had one, and it proved a perfect complement for flared jeans. As a fabric, the muslin or cotton that was originally used for pressing curds was refreshingly easy-care. The crinkles meant that ironing was a thing of the past, but, as one wearer recalls, "you had to be careful with your wash temperature – if it was too hot, it shrank!". The baby-doll style here was a real favourite, as was this ethnic, loose-fitting embroidered silk shirt, one of a growing number of brightly-coloured fashion imports from India.

Cheesecloth shirt	£20–25	$35–45
Silk shirt	£15–20	$25–35

← Before the Oil Crisis of 1973 it was still tempting, reasonably affordable and a real challenge to experiment with plastics. The French designer André Courrèges (b.1923) was one of those who led the way with this wet-look leatherette coat. Almost as a precursor to what was to come with Punk style, he turned functional fastenings into decorative details by adding a bold white zip above each pocket. Watch out for wear and tear on original examples as the plastic coating can crack around the stitched areas.

£250–450	$450–810

→ When the BBC refused to play The Sex Pistols' hit *God Save the Queen* in Silver Jubilee year (1977), international media coverage brought Punk style into most suburban homes and, at the same time, encouraged top fashion designers to adopt a toned-down version of this radical look. The British designer Zandra Rhodes (b.1940), who made this dress, translated street style Punk into high-class evening wear by incorporating safety pins, diamanté studs and hanging chains. She labelled it her Conceptual Chic collection (1977) and believed it was "aesthetic, sexy and seductive". The writer and broadcaster Janet Street-Porter, who was a great fan of Rhodes's designs in the 1970s, wore this dress.

£400–600	$720–1,100

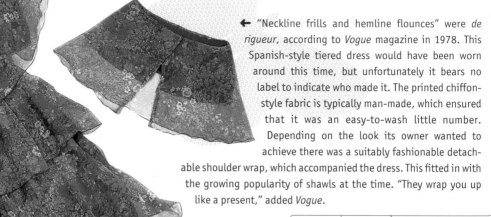

← "Neckline frills and hemline flounces" were *de rigueur*, according to *Vogue* magazine in 1978. This Spanish-style tiered dress would have been worn around this time, but unfortunately it bears no label to indicate who made it. The printed chiffon-style fabric is typically man-made, which ensured that it was an easy-to-wash little number. Depending on the look its owner wanted to achieve there was a suitably fashionable detach-able shoulder wrap, which accompanied the dress. This fitted in with the growing popularity of shawls at the time. "They wrap you up like a present," added *Vogue*.

£45–50	$80–90

"Neckline frills and hemline flounces"

→ Laura Ashley (1925–85) had come a long way from her humble beginnings in the 1950s, when she printed scarves and napkins on her kitchen table for the British department stores John Lewis and Heal's. By the end of the 1970s there were 25 Laura Ashley stores in the United Kingdom plus a host more in Europe and the United States. Taking the 1970s trend for revivalism to heart, Ashley breathed new life into Victorian and Edwardian floral prints. Her designs, which turned grown women into country maids, were widely copied, as the skirt on the far right shows. Always check labels to uncover the real thing.

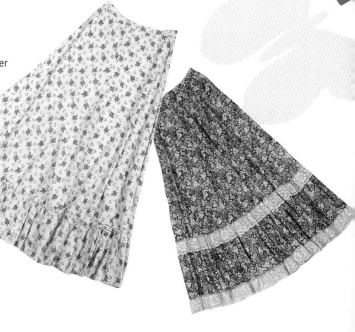

Laura Ashley skirt	£30–35	$55–65
Hand-sewn skirt	£35–40	$65–75

← Jeans "add up to instant chic" said Barbara Griggs, fashion editor of the *Daily Mail* newspaper, and flares like these were an essential part of dressing in the 1970s. Traditionally classed as men's workwear, jeans had moved on apace and were now accepted as fashion classics for both sexes. One wearer remembers distressing hers so that they "looked really frayed and used". A close look at the metal fly-buttons reveal that these decorated jeans, complete with hang-loose "hashish" patch on the back pocket, were made by Levi Strauss & Co. Personalizing flares with badges or fabric offcuts as here was definitely "in", and Levi Strauss was inundated by a huge response when it sponsored a Denim Art Contest in 1973. Apart from denim there was a strong demand for non-iron flares in easy-care man-made fabric, like this vivid orange pair in polyester, with a matching belt and feature buckle, from New Criss.

£50–70	$90–125	*New Criss flares*
£230–250	$415–450	*Personalized jeans*

"jeans had moved on apace and were now accepted as fashion classics for both sexes"

→ The swirling patterns of this chiffon fabric echo the whole flow of the trouser suit, which a few decades before would have been deemed unacceptable for women's wear. Thanks to designers such as Yves Saint Laurent (b.1936), who crossed gender barriers in the 1960s by dressing women in men's suits, the trouser suit was a key element of the fashionable woman's wardrobe in the 1970s. "Now that the longer line is with us again," said *Homes & Gardens* magazine in 1971, "suits are very much a proposition." Although it looks like the work of the Italian Emilio Pucci, neither part carries the "Emilio" signature, which reduces the value.

£100–120	$180–215

disco diva

It's "Paa-rty! Paa-rty!" announced *Rolling Stone* magazine when it looked at the boom in discothèque rock in 1973. What it witnessed was "a rapidly spreading social phenomenon" which had "a strong influence on the music people listen to and buy". With the disco cult came a new style of dressing. Parquet dancefloors dictated the pace, and New York's Studio 54, which opened in 1977, became a Mecca for stars and their fans who wanted to "get on down". Chart hits like *Hot Stuff* by Donna Summer, *He's the Greatest Dancer* from Sister Sledge, and Sylvester's *You make me feel (mighty real)* confirmed that if you wanted to join in you had to be able to move. So slippery synthetics came into their own, making even the tightest boogie routine possible. Shimmering Lurex and sequins reflected the disco's classic mirror-ball lights. The dance craze and the fashions it spawned became mainstream with the release in 1977 of the film *Saturday Night Fever*, which brought disco to the masses with the Bee Gees, who got everyone dancing to *Night Fever* and *Stayin' Alive*.

↓ The tight-fitting catsuits of the 1960s, as sported by Emma Peel in the British television series *The Avengers*, gave way to baggy bellbottoms a decade later. This all-in-one suit carries the distinguished Jean Allen label, which enhances its value. In the 1950s the London-based designer gained a following for her New-Look A-line dresses. Glitzy silver, made possible by the advent of new synthetic metallic threads, was the ultimate disco colour, and this was certainly a high-style outfit. Apart from being dance-floor wear, it was a look that popped up in countless 1970s movies.

£75–150 | $135–270

➡ Slinky silk-feel shirts that were actually made from 100% man-made materials reflected the glamorous 1970s. They were inexpensive, eye-catching and distinctly unisex. Sally James, from the popular British children's television show *Tiswas*, first screened by ATV in 1974, recalls how girls "always wanted to dress like men … it was cross-dressing in a really light, fun kind of way". Synthetic materials may have been easy to clean but they were not made to last, so always check the condition carefully.

Each | £20–25 | $35–45

⬅ The tube top, colloquially branded the "boob tube", was modern, ultra-fitted and perfectly suited to a night out on the town. The cutting-edge British designer Anne Tyrell was fascinated by the 1970s' "new and directional fabrics". Combining a love for antique clothes and the sequins that adorned 1920s and 1930s dresses, she came up with a style you could wear without support. Her innovative design did not intentionally encourage women to burn their bras, but it was hugely influential as it filtered down to the street through less expensive imitations. An "Anne Tyrell at John Marks" label indicates the pedigree of this outfit.

£35–40 | $65–75

"glitzy silver ... was the ultimate disco colour"

➡ The design of this vest-style top owed as much to the burgeoning interest in fitness in the 1970s as it did to the need to be cool on the dance floor. Here metallic thread runs through the acetate fabric to give a glitzy look that would have been picked up in an instant under bright disco lights. For its wearer, as *Vogue* magazine confirmed in 1976, dressing was clearly about "all out glamour to outshine everything".

£15–20 | $25–35

➜ A pair of dark-velvet flared trousers became a staple fashion item in the 1970s. Some women teamed them with lurex cardigans or skimpy body-line wraparound tops, while others opted for something altogether more floaty, such as the batwing-sleeve blouses shown on the opposite page. In many cases the waistline dropped to just below the belly-button for that ultra-cool, hip-hugging look. The recent revival of the flared style in contemporary fashion has meant that original examples from the 1970s have become increasingly desirable.

| £40–45 | $75–80 |

⬅ "It was gossamer thin and so comfortable to wear," recalls the owner of this silver-and-brown lamé dress, bought from the upmarket British high-street store Richard Shops. "I was a fan of Biba's purple eyeshadow, and I remember dancing in it with that dark plummy colour around my eyes, loads of mascara and my long hair parted in the middle." The scooped neckline remained a favourite throughout the 1970s, especially with smaller women because, along with the obligatory platform shoes, it helped to accentuate their height.

| £40–60 | $75–110 |

➜ A glamorous take on the classic bomber-jacket style, which returned with a passion this decade. Followers of fashion often opted for the blouson look as a mark of support for their pop heroes, and these jackets, particularly when they were made in sateen fabric, became known as "tour" jackets. This one, by the Canadian label Adam & Eve, has an elasticated waist and is made from leather, which is given a lift with its shiny gold coating.

| £150–250 | $270–450 |

→ Loose-fitting batwing sleeves grew out of a revived interest in ethnic clothes, and worked best when the fabric was, as *Homes & Gardens* magazine said, "flowing and floating". The blouse on the left, by Carole Lee, is made from ultra-fine mohair, interwoven with metallic thread. The silver blouse on the right is typically Abba-esque, and its angel-wing style and colour seemed to be a favourite with the band's blonde-haired singer, Agnetha Faltskog. She chose to wear her versions of this blouse with white flares.

Carole Lee blouse	£50–60	$90–110
Silver blouse	£55–65	$95–120

"it exposed a good helping of bare flesh"

← The halter neck dominated fashion during the 1970s, and found itself incorporated into everything from bikinis to evening dresses. "This had quite thick ties," says its owner, "the idea was that I'd tie them round my neck and let the tails hang down my back." In many ways the sexy plunging back that resulted from the halter-neck style evoked the sleek lines of the French designer Madeleine Vionnet's bias-cut creations of the 1930s. One of the advantages of this neckline was that it exposed a good helping of bare flesh, which meant that 1970s sun worshippers could really show off their tans. This dress is made from non-iron polyester, and its owner regularly found it an essential for holiday travel. "It was light to pack," she recalls, "and when I took it out of my suitcase it was ready to pop on."

£25–30	$45–55

punk style

Social upheaval and workers' strikes in 1970s Britain encouraged bored working-class teenagers to rebel. Disillusioned by the status quo, disenfranchised youngsters called for social change through support of anti-establishment rock music. Bands like The Damned, The Clash and The Sex Pistols (the latter branded "the foul-mouthed yobs" by the *Daily Mail* newspaper) became both idols and voices for these teenagers. "We managed to offend all the people we were fed up with," reflected The Sex Pistols' manager, Malcolm McLaren. Clothing was a key expression of their irreverence, leading to the birth of Punk style. The artificially torn, stained, safety-pinned and chained look came from poverty on the streets. Supporters who saw Punk outfits worn on stage by the Pistols' lead singer, Johnny Rotten (John Lydon), trawled London for their own versions. Shops like Seditionaries and Boy were a Mecca for kids with short dyed and spiked hair. As one wearer remembers: "Punk was an experience. You didn't wear these clothes to behave – you wore them to misbehave." So original Punk clothing with trademark labels in good condition is a rarity that is prized by collectors.

→ Elongated arms and bodies – the "wrong-size look" – are a distinctive feature of Punk garments. Knitted mohair sweaters like these were designed by Vivienne Westwood (b.1941) and Malcolm McLaren (b.1946) but carry no labels. Although they came in a variety of patterns and colours, ranging from this diagonal theme to classic red-and-white stripes, the figure-hugging outline remained the same. This survivor, complete with holes, is more special than most – Johnny Rotten wore it. Without the personality link it would be worth around £400 or $600, but its association with The Sex Pistols' lead singer means it is far more valuable.

| £3,000–3,500 | $5,400–6,300 |

← Parachute tops were worn by Punk bands and their supporters. The harness without its parachute seems to reflect the sense of hopelessness felt by gangs of rebellious youths. By 1979, when this jacket was made, the street revolution was falling apart as non-conformist Punk started to become mainstream. The safety-pinned look was even absorbed into high fashion thanks to the British designer Zandra Rhodes (b.1940). An "establishment" newspaper, the *Daily Mail*, added insult to injury with a feature on "How to turn yourself into a Punk". Then came the death of The Sex Pistols' bassist-turned-singer, Sid Vicious, on 2 February 1979. The words "No future" and "99% is shit" printed over the denim fabric sum up the strength of feeling.

| £600–1,200 | $1,100–2,150 |

← These T-shirt designs, created by Vivienne Westwood, Malcolm McLaren and their art director, Jamie Reid (b.1940), were originally for sale in the King's Road shop Seditionaries. True Punk had to be controversial, and what better way to spark an outcry than to print an image of Queen Elizabeth II, then celebrating her Silver Jubilee, with a safety pin through her nose? The Chaos T-shirt lists life's horrors, as the makers saw them: "famous personalities", "the job that you hate but are too scared to pack in", and worst of all, "the suburbs"! Those who flocked to the shop could have bought any one of 25 designs printed on a variety of plain shirts – from cotton like this to a muslin long-sleeved shirt, priced at £6.50. Authentic examples have both seams and labels on the outside.

Chaos T-shirt	£200–400	$360–720
God Save the Queen T-shirt	£200–400	$360–720

→ Tight-legged tartan "Bondage Trousers" were part of the McLaren/Westwood unisex look and were boldly announced to the public as suitable for "soldiers, prostitutes, dykes and punks". Although they look as if they have been thrown together, with their flannel "bum flap", random zips and leg strap, like a great deal of original Punk clothing these trousers are extremely well made. The seams were overstitched to prevent fraying, and only the highest quality zips were used. This early pair dates from around 1975 when the McLaren/Westwood shop at 430 King's Road in London was called Sex, before it transformed into Seditionaries a year later. Watch out for cheap period copies – this design in particular spawned many – which suffer from the use of cheap fabric and poor quality stitching.

£400–600	$720–1,100

lingerie and swimwear

Torn between a desire to be both sexually liberated and sexy, women opted for a varied range of underwear this decade. Much of it was inspired by trends in fashion. So, for instance, the return of the waistline brought a revival of the girdle, albeit in a form that was "strong but almost invisible". A new arrival in 1972 was the halter-neck bra – a godsend for all those with matching bodice necklines. The slimline fit of trousers, jerseys and dresses sparked a quest for seamfree underwear that would not leave any visible lines. And as gossamer-sheer fabrics took off, the bright colours of 1960s bras gave way to more muted flesh tones. Sun-drenched package holidays became more accessible, and what you wore on the beach counted. New styles included the "one shoulder" swimsuit, ultra high-cut leg lines and the "identi-print bikini and swimsuit". Synthetic fibres were widely used, even for stretch cottons incorporating Lycra that arrived as part of the fitness craze at the end of the decade.

← From the man who shocked the world in 1964 with his topless bathing suit came this revealing swimsuit in 1971. The Californian designer Rudi Gernreich (1922–85) lived up to his image as "the farthest-out of all American dress designers" when he styled this Roualt bathing costume for the Harmon Knitwear company. Here he plays with the notion of physical freedom by revealing and covering parts of the body. Although Gernreich's designs were more conceptual than mainstream (hence their rarity and value) they were precursors of the unsupported swimsuits that became a trademark of this decade. In the late 1970s he moved swimwear on again with his thong bikini.

| £1,500–1,700 | $2,700–3,000 |

← The owner of two of these bikinis (far and near left) was so taken with the designs that she bought them both. For the larger-busted woman, the halter-neck shape was extremely flattering, and it persisted throughout the 1970s. The bikini in the middle is another gem from the Italian designer Emilio Pucci (1914–92). Firmly associated with jet-set travel, having designed airline uniforms, he naturally progressed to developing a line of luxury bikinis. Look out for his distinctive "Emilio" signature intertwined in the fabric.

Fan bikini	£10–15	$18–25
Pucci bikini	£70–80	$125–145
Striped bikini	£10–15	$18–25

"perfect for tight-fitting jerseys"

→ The battle for support this decade headed in the direction of bras that were discreet but still uplifting. Gossard was at the forefront of developments with its Glossies collection of seamless bras that proved perfect for tight-fitting jerseys. The underwired white halter-neck bra by Berlei and the strapless black bra were specifically designed to wear with fashionable dress styles. The front-fastening burgundy-lace bra followed the romantic look that re-appeared in the 1970s, spearheaded by Janet Reger's frilly underwear. It was probably part of a set that included matching lace-embroidered knickers and a pared-down suspender girdle. As the decade progressed, cotton, albeit woven with Lycra for stretch, gradually made a come-back in underwear, as seen here in these cotton knickers by the Italian firm Primizia.

Bras (each)	£9–15	$16–25
Knickers	£6–8	$11–15

FASHION

hats, shoes and bags

"Dressing down", as championed by *Vogue* in the 1970s, relied on a fresh breed of accessories. As style took a more relaxed line, so did classics like hats. Wide, floppy brims replaced anything formal and stiff, and Ali MacGraw started a craze for crochet-knitted skullcaps after wearing one in the film *Love Story*. "The ultimate accessory", according to *Nova* magazine in 1974, was a headscarf, which you could wear "twisted, plaited, knotted or wrapped around the head and neck". Soft suede and leather belts were favourites for gathering tough knits or even silky *crêpe-de-chine* shirts around the waist, and flung over every shoulder was a large hold-all handbag. *Nova* claimed that "to look magnificently decadent you need clumpy high-heeled shoes". The chunky look of 1940s footwear reappeared, appealing to a unisex market whose members' stature rose in some cases by a stunning 8in (20cm). In 1974 the rise of the training shoe was complete when Nike's Waffle trainer became the bestselling shoe in the United States.

← This floppy felt hat was made as the 1970s arrived and hat wearing was becoming optional rather than the necessity it had been a couple of decades earlier. Fedora styles like this one, with its broad brim, were definitely unisex, and you would be as likely to see one topping a midi raincoat and thigh-length boots as above a pair of hipster trousers and an Afghan coat. The important German milliner Otto Lucas (1903–71), who designed privately for clients such as the Duchess of Windsor, styled this hat for London's Fortnum & Mason store, so it was definitely top of the range. For collectors, the all-important label is there to prove it.

£40–60 | $75–110

← Glittering sequins went hand in hand with disco dancing, and what better way to sport them than on your head. This was a look that music fans snapped up after the pop group Abba paraded sparkling skullcaps similar to this red one on their album covers and on the stage. The tight-fitting nature of such hats was offset by long hair, softly layered and curled away from the face at the sides with the help of a few rollers. Neither of these hats has any labels to indicate who made it, reducing their value, but both are in pristine condition, which always appeals to vintage costume enthusiasts.

£30–35 | $55–65 | *Each*

92

← It may have looked the part, but this telephone bag was not exactly useful on the dance floor. Stylish, yes, but practical, no! A zipper pocket inside holds the all-important wall cord restricting its use to within a few steps of a telephone socket, so unless you could move the wall to the disco floor (unlikely) you could not make or receive any calls. The British telephone system was not ready for this quirky vinyl gem but the American system was. Those who did buy one (and there were not many made, hence its collectability) could choose between this ivory colour and a delightful black faux-crocodile version. Far more practical was this glamorous gold clutch bag – a style for the 1970s – or this 1950s-style shoulder bag and wallet set which takes advantage of new developments in plastic.

Telephone bag	£1,350–1,650	$2,350–2,900
Purple set	£18–20	$30–35
Gold clutch bag	£20–25	$35–45

"Stylish, yes, but practical, no!"

→ Random zips and buckles were signatures of Punk clothing, as they were embellishments that looked thrown together and firmly anti-fashion. You could not get a better example of Punk style in footwear than these "bondage boots". They were sold in Seditionaries (which carried the slogan "clothes for heroes"), the McLaren/Westwood shop on London's King's Road, a move on from the couple's previous Punk venture, Sex, in 1976. This is tough 1970s street style at its best, so it may seem surprising that such footwear has survived in good condition. One reason is that, despite its down-at-heel image, Seditionaries produced well-made clothes and shoes. Less expensive copies were available from other outlets, but few have stood the test of time.

£500–800	$900–400

← "New hair colouring and conditioning techniques make possible rapid colour changes," said *Nova* in 1973, so women were far more likely to flaunt their hairstyle than conceal it beneath a hat in the 1970s. Despite this, die-hards clung to tradition, albeit in a far more relaxed way. Rigid brims became floppy, as these three hats demonstrate. Fabrics and patterns reflected the spirit of the age, and the ethnic look crept into styling. Nostalgia also played a big part in 1970s headgear, and just as dresses and suits drew their inspiration variously from the 1920s and 1940s, so too did hats.

£15–25	$25–45	*Each*

"big and beautiful was in"

→ With the arrival of the "midi" length came calf-hugging platform boots. Worn beneath a belted raincoat with a hem that finished half way down the leg, they were seen as the utmost in sophistication. Improved zipper technology, thanks partly to the expansion of the Japanese firm YKK, which built its first factory in the United States in 1974, meant that they were easy to slip on and off. Biba chose a fashionable "Blue Bottle" coloured cotton for the boots above, while other manufacturers opted for vibrant dyed or high-gloss patent leathers. Examine the boots inside to spot makers' labels, such as Biba's trademark gold logo, which add to their value.

Biba boots	£250–300	$450–540
Leather boots	£25–45	$45–80

← When it came to 1970s handbags, small and delicate was out and big and beautiful was in. Films like *Annie Hall* ushered in larger holdall-style bags, designed to carry more than just bare necessities, slung over the shoulder with a long strap rather than neatly suspended from the wrist by a stiff handle. The look was altogether more casual. Part of the effect came from the soft leather and suede used. Italian firms like Fendi, which made this stylish sunray bag, excelled at stitching leather, appliqué-style, to give an ethnic feel. Belts were a must-have accessory, and this one would have been worn tied round a cable-knit jersey or a loose shirt to emphasize the waist.

£15–20	$25–35	Horsehair bag
£5–8	$9–15	Fendi belt
£18–20	$30–35	Fendi bag

→ Retro styling touched every aspect of 1970s fashion, including shoes. The chunky heels and soles of the 1940s returned, this time mixed with the feel and elevation of traditional Roman sandals, complete with block toes. "They made me feel far more powerful and in control," recalls one platform-sole addict who stood a mere 5ft (152cm) without them. Neither of these pairs carries any maker's marks, so there is no hint as to who made them, which reduces their value.

Each pair	£20–40	$35–75

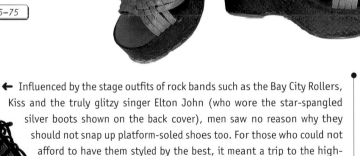

← Influenced by the stage outfits of rock bands such as the Bay City Rollers, Kiss and the truly glitzy singer Elton John (who wore the star-spangled silver boots shown on the back cover), men saw no reason why they should not snap up platform-soled shoes too. For those who could not afford to have them styled by the best, it meant a trip to the high-street shoe store where lace-ups like these were on offer. "My first pair cost £11.99," says one former 1970s teenager. But this was equivalent to a third of a week's wages, so youngsters still had to save up to buy such trendy accessories.

Each pair	£25–45	$45–80

cosmetics

"Some women give up wearing make-up because of women's lib – others in spite of it," announced *Nova* magazine in 1974. Those still opting for the trappings of adornment moved away from the Space Age look of the 1960s towards make-up that accentuated natural features. Nostalgia for past eras brought back vivid rouge lips and cheeks, enhanced by "luscious" coloured lipsticks and blushers. "All out glamour", as described by *Vogue* in 1976, arrived with the decade's hip cosmetics – lip gloss and coloured mascara. The optical specialist Bausch & Lomb unveiled the world's first soft contact lenses in 1971, but priced at upwards of £75 or $115 a pair they remained highly exclusive. Must-have scents such as Charlie were aimed at sexually liberated, independent working girls, although whether those who wore it really fitted in with Revlon's slick advertising is questionable. Men, meanwhile, were enjoying a new array of "designer" colognes bought for the brand rather than any revitalizing quality. Today collectors snap up original 1970s perfume bottles, particularly those still full of scent with their packaging intact.

← "It will diffuse through its incandescent powers ... the things that most appeal to the heart, the charms of seduction, which give birth to passionate life," said Yves Saint Laurent (b.1936) in 1977 at the launch of his revolutionary perfume Opium. Its name conjured up pure addiction, and its spicy eastern notes broke away from the subtle florals that dominated the industry at the time. The photographer Helmut Newton shot an advertising campaign with the model Jerry Hall lying with her head back in rapture. Collectors adore both the Japanese-style inro bottle and the red-and-gold packaging, designed by Pierre Dinand.

£12–15 $20–25

← Charlie was without doubt *the* perfume of the decade. Its creators, the American cosmetics giant Revlon, designed it for a new breed of woman – the young working girl in tune with feminism. Promoted as "the gorgeous, sexy, young fragrance" when it came out in 1973, Charlie was a "must-have" which went hand-in-hand with the growing popularity of all things American, from denim to soft drinks. Keen to keep the new scent under wraps, Revlon gave it a code name, "Cosmos", during development, and only a handful of technicians knew exactly what it contained. By the mid-1970s it was the world's number one fragrance, and from it came a full cosmetics line that is still a bestseller today.

£8–12 $15–20

← Hairstyles needed constant attention in the 1970s. Even the hippie look with long locks parted in the centre required regular grooming to keep it in place, so what better way to tackle knots than with this Mod Kooky Comb? "Take it anywhere", said the packaging, and "get into the scene". Whether it was a real "his and hers" fashion asset hanging round the neck was doubtful, but the flip side did have a very useful mirror. Most of those that survive are not mounted in their original packaging like this example.

£18–20	$30–35

→ Fans of groovy new cuts like the layered and curled "Farrah Fawcett style" were stuck with far more regular hair care. "Like Farrah, you may need to shampoo and set your hair every day," one hairdressing magazine thoughtfully advised. Manufacturers quickly responded with a range of "convenience" products – shampoos with follow-on conditioners and sure set hairsprays that were easy to use at home. Specific rinses for tinted hair were also available for the growing band of women who opted for milder colouring formulas. "These new tints lift the hair without taking the pigment from it," said *Nova* magazine.

Each	£6–8	$11–15

← With the promise of unleashing "fragrances so powerful and appealing to women that you had to be careful how you use them", Hai Karate after shave, by the British firm Unicliffe Ltd, was a hot seller. Medallion man raised his sex appeal with this splash-on cologne branded "as mystical and masculine as karate itself". It was promoted by a run of memorable television advertisements promising a "cram course on self-defence in every package!". The aptly-named Wild Country, an "all-purpose cologne for men" from Avon, relied on similar marketing ideas. From Paco Rabanne came the up-market Paco Rabanne Pour Homme after shave in 1973. Its blend of rich spicy herbs made it ideal for evening wear.

£10–12	$18–20	Paco Rabanne Pour Homme
£10–12	$18–20	Hai Karate
£8–10	$15–18	Wild Country

jewellery

A bizarre mix of "all out glamour", heralded by *Vogue*, and "dressing down" led to a diverse range of jewellery in the 1970s. For the newly independent working woman wishing to emphasize her position in a man's world there were decadent and showy accessories. Designers such as Kenneth Jay Lane came up with fashionable lines of *faux* baubles to rival the brightest kipper ties. With this new-found glitzy style came empowerment – a trouser-suited lady ready to run the show. Meanwhile, other jewellers played a simpler card, more in tune with the craft revival. Nature offered plenty of inspiration in terms of both organic shapes and previously underrated semi-precious stones. Tiger's eye, coral and black onyx were deemed as acceptable as rubies and diamonds. In keeping with a retro feel in fashion, Renaissance-style pendants now became *de rigueur*. It was also time to experiment, as the British designer Edward de Large showed with his remarkable titanium jewellery, which seemed to be three-dimensional.

← This earring set came from the man who revived costume jewellery, the American designer Kenneth Jay Lane. "For a young woman real jewellery is very ageing, and people wonder where she got it," he said. "An older woman who has an enormous amount of valuable jewels feels younger wearing costume jewellery." His sumptuous creations undoubtedly made both feel like a million dollars. Cast lion heads were a trademark. Here they are combined with richly coloured plastics that slot in place to resemble doorknockers. In essence the look was one of power – jewellery for a woman who was not to be messed with.

| £75–85 | $135–155 |

← While some designers went for all-out flamboyance, others, like Mikela Nau who crafted this decorative pin brooch, opted to experiment with materials in far more simple shapes. This is very much a hand-crafted piece where Nau has explored the look of oxidized silver using two very basic geometric outlines. The results are an understated elegance and a brooch that would have been admired for its cutting-edge design. The fact that the person who crafted this piece is known, thanks to the tiny maker's mark, does add to its value.

| £100–150 | $180–270 |

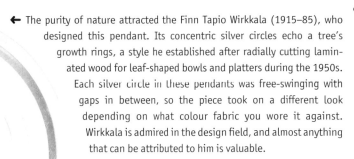

← The purity of nature attracted the Finn Tapio Wirkkala (1915–85), who designed this pendant. Its concentric silver circles echo a tree's growth rings, a style he established after radially cutting laminated wood for leaf-shaped bowls and platters during the 1950s. Each silver circle in these pendants was free-swinging with gaps in between, so the piece took on a different look depending on what colour fabric you wore it against. Wirkkala is admired in the design field, and almost anything that can be attributed to him is valuable.

| £300–400 | $540–720 |

→ "This is a great favourite of mine bought from a jewellery party," recalls the owner of this pendant necklace. A version of the classic 1970s Tupperware get-together, the jewellery party was a place for women to take advantage of up-to-the-minute styles at prices that were affordable. Pendants were trendy during this decade, and so were whole ranges of semi-precious stones. In this case the reflective properties of the mother-of-pearl insert were "memorably alluring". However, this is not a top-of-the-range designer piece, so its value is relatively low, but items like this are sought after by collectors of 1970s style.

| £15–20 | $25–35 |

← Silver was a great favourite for jewellery designers in the 1970s because it was malleable and could take on nature's organic shapes quite easily. This brilliantly sculptured pendant and necklace are both by the Finnish designer Pentti Sarpaneva, who was one of the great masters working in silver at this time. To get the overall design to flow as freely as a stream of water was by no means easy. It would have taken many hours of close work to achieve the look. And with such fine workmanship and construction it is no wonder that these pieces command high prices today.

Pendant (top) | £300–400 | $540–720 |
Necklace (bottom) | £400–500 | $720–900 |

menswear

The peacock revolution that kick-started unisex dressing during the 1960s had embraced mainstream men's fashion by the 1970s. Gone were the days when colour and floral patterns were aimed only at women and young men. The key to smart dressing for men of all ages was the figure-hugging, tailored-cut suit jacket. Trousers were close-fitting around the hips but gloriously flared at the ankles. Lapels spread, as did shirt collars, which became so wide that those who opted for a tie were left with little choice beyond the broad "kipper", or a cravat. "Leisureman" opted for a relaxed casual look, and open-necked shirts, with or without frills, and polo-neck jerseys were essentials, particularly with zip-up wool blousons or belted safari-style jackets. For young people, the Vietnam War took fashion in a new direction. Partly in sympathy for those who were drafted and partly as a signal of defiance against the horrors of conflict, rebellious teenagers on both sides of the Atlantic turned to combat gear. In the United Kingdom the look included parka jackets with Doc Marten boots, and was bound up with the alienation felt by the young.

↑ With the more relaxed attitude to dressing outside work, the polo-neck jersey was a key fashion item in the 1970s. High around the neck, it dispensed with the need for a tie yet still looked stylish. If you wanted the smart-casual feel, you chose a thick-ribbed polo-neck to wear under a sports or blouson jacket. For something more upbeat you opted for a thinner polo-neck, like this cream cotton one by Double Act, worn beneath a V-neck sweater. The green polo neck on the left, with its popular striped pattern, is by Ditto Ditto.

Each | £10–15 | $18–25

← In an age where blue jeans in varying shades were king, rival manufacturers had to keep ahead of the game. Here Levi Strauss & Co. takes the distressed look one step further by making flares (known as loons because of their wide leg) from stitched patches, a technique often associated with leather. It was a look that could easily be copied, as many discovered. "I used to cut up my old pairs for patches and inserts for the flares," recalls one 1970s teenager.

£30–35 | $55–65

➔ As the 1970s moved on, working-class kids with few prospects felt increasingly sidelined by society. One of the few safe havens they could count on was the army surplus store. There you would find racks of parka or "snorkel" jackets similar to the one featured here. Historically they were made from caribou or seal and worn by the Eskimos in the Arctic. When the military snapped up their wrap-up style as essential combat gear for cold climates, waterproof synthetic fabrics were used instead. Sage green with a distinctive orange lining was one of the most popular colour combinations for such jackets.

| £25–30 | $45 55 |

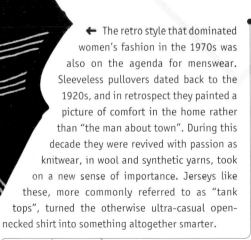

← The retro style that dominated women's fashion in the 1970s was also on the agenda for menswear. Sleeveless pullovers dated back to the 1920s, and in retrospect they painted a picture of comfort in the home rather than "the man about town". During this decade they were revived with passion as knitwear, in wool and synthetic yarns, took on a new sense of importance. Jerseys like these, more commonly referred to as "tank tops", turned the otherwise ultra-casual open-necked shirt into something altogether smarter.

| £20–30 | $35–55 | *Each*

← "Window-pane checks", as *Vogue* magazine described these patterns, were more than hip for tailored sports blazers. The British high-quality fashion label Burberry led the way when it used its classic lining check pattern for a tweed-jacket fabric, revealing a new vivid-blue colourway for men in 1976. The jacket on the right, labelled Val Cassi, is made from cotton seersucker fabric, a material which had been traditionally associated with women's clothing. The jacket on the left is by the British manufacturer Charles Baker. Both of these designs stand out on their own, so it is no wonder that fashion magazines firmly ruled out wearing anything other than a plain polo-neck jersey underneath.

| £30–40 | $55–75 | Val Cassi jacket |
| £25–35 | $45–65 | Charles Baker jacket |

"Feminine-looking garments were totally acceptable…"

→ "Medallion man" would have been completely at ease in the white shirt on the right with its extrovert jabots. But if he did not want to opt for the open-necked look, then, as pop idol Captain Beefheart showed on his 1972 album (see p.121), it went just as well with a black dog-collar. Colour was a key part of male dressing, as the vivid blue of the lacy shirt on the left shows. Both shirts are made from a drip-dry polyester/cotton mix. Feminine-looking garments were totally acceptable for smart middle-class men. They were just another extension of the androgynous fashion that was cutting through the masculine wardrobe.

| £25–30 | $45–55 | Each |

→ Few television series summed up suburban man's fashion at this time better than the BBC's *Whatever Happened to the Likely Lads?*, screened in 1973–74. In a continuation of the successful 1960s comedy *The Likely Lads* we followed not only Bob's marriage to "the dreaded Thelma" but also his department-store fashion. This up-to-the-minute burgundy suit cut from the finest wool/polyester mix is just the sort of outfit Bob (as played by actor Rodney Bewes) would have worn. Its slimline tailored style echoed the return of the waist in women's clothing, and the flared trousers reveal the influence that hippie style had on conventional dress. Needless to say, it was a look that was perfect for a young slim build but was pretty disastrous otherwise.

£40–60	$75–110

← Ties made a comeback in the 1970s after being deemed far too traditional by anti-establishment dressers in the 1960s. They grew in width to complement the wide-pointed shirt collars that had taken fashion by storm. Men found that there was a wide variety of ties to choose from. The selection here includes a pre-knotted bright orange tie and a purple Hatton Dandy tie, both of which are made from synthetic polyester instead of silk. There was also a broad range of novelty prints available, like this aviation-print tie from British Home Stores, as well as challenging patterns along the lines of this diagonally striped tie by Casual Aire.

Purple Hatton Dandy tie	£8–12	$15–20
Pre-knotted tie	£8–12	$15–20
Aviation tie	£6–8	$11–15
Casual Aire tie	£8–12	$15–20

← Western fashion took many of its cues from the Afro-Caribbean community during the 1970s. The image of the cool black man-about-town striding confidently in his leather-and-suede clothing soon crossed over to traditional tailoring, as revealed in the cut, colour and style of this suit by the British outfitters Cordoba. It is made from deep-pink suede, a colour that two decades earlier would have raised plenty of eyebrows. A suede suit like this would have been expensive but still within the reach of those who wanted to be truly funky.

£100–300 | $180–540

→ Boot-cut flares were classed as casual hippie wear in the late 1960s, but by now they had become mainstream fashion. Whether you were a slick-dressing executive complete with a fashionable Zappa-esque moustache, or a working-class man at home on a building site, a pair of flares was the new standard. The trousers on the left by Garland have a thick waistband and double buttons, which accentuates their close fit over hips and waist. Made from a polyester/rayon mix, they proudly advertise the fact that they are suitable for the tumble dryer.

Each | £20–25 | $35–45

← Stylish man, as *Vogue* magazine identified him in 1976, wore a blouson jacket. The look was similar in many ways to the classic wartime bomber jacket, but a shorter cut revealed rather than concealed the hips. This checked blouson with poppers as fasteners was made by Canadian-based Liberty Sportswear Ltd. Its stretch waistband and cuffs are typical style features that persisted whatever the material. Although this example is not reversible, many blouson jackets of the period were.

£55–65 | $95–120

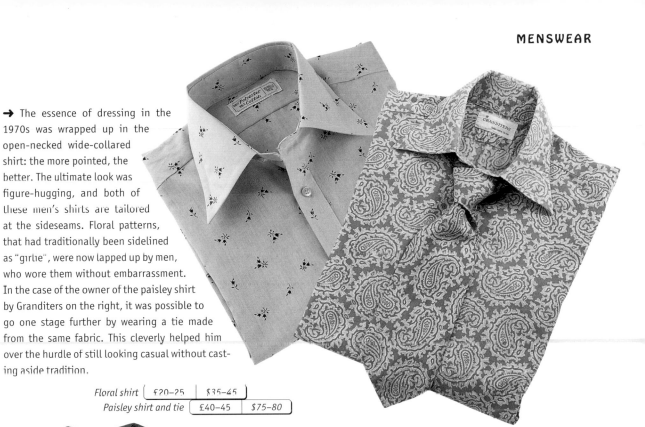

→ The essence of dressing in the 1970s was wrapped up in the open-necked wide-collared shirt: the more pointed, the better. The ultimate look was figure-hugging, and both of these men's shirts are tailored at the sideseams. Floral patterns, that had traditionally been sidelined as "girlie", were now lapped up by men, who wore them without embarrassment. In the case of the owner of the paisley shirt by Granditers on the right, it was possible to go one stage further by wearing a tie made from the same fabric. This cleverly helped him over the hurdle of still looking casual without casting aside tradition.

Floral shirt	£20–25	$35–45
Paisley shirt and tie	£40–45	$75–80

"a new style based on classic safari clothes was born"

← When the French fashion guru Yves Saint Laurent (b.1936) launched his "Saharienne" collection for men in 1968, a new style based on classic safari clothes was born. As the look filtered down to the streets in the 1970s, shirts and jackets gained button-down epaulettes and large patch pockets, plus a distinctive nipped-in style with the help of a belt around the waist. The unlabelled brown-leather jacket on the right was a close match to the smart but casual clothing worn by CI5 agent Bodie, as played by Lewis Collins in the television series *The Professionals* (1977–83). Would-be tough-guy fans would have snapped it up to match their screen hero.

£45–50	$80–90	Safari jacket
£50–80	$90–145	Leather jacket

Despite
spiralling oil
prices, workers' strikes
and the rumblings of the
Watergate scandal, there was endless
entertainment to be had for those who wanted
to party. The new high-fidelity systems were
tuned in to pop sounds from greats like Elton
John, Supertramp, Bob Marley and The Sex
Pistols in a decade of musical
diversity – Glam Rock ran
alongside reggae

leisure

and Punk nestled up to disco. Headlines broke the news of "Rollermania" and "Abbamania" as fans clamoured to snap up any number of mementoes of their favourite group, in the shape of look-alike dolls, made-to-match clothing or coloured vinyls. Television and films also brought new stars to light, and toy firms did their best to match these screen heroes in miniature. Just like their parents, children moved rapidly into the electronic age this decade with the very first video games, playable from the comfort of the living-room sofa. Outside they took to the streets on a new line of wheels, including the classic Chopper bicycle, a run of streamlined skateboards, and slip-on but reluctantly slip-off roller-skates.

toys and dolls

Driven by statistics revealing that traditional toys no longer appealed to 12 to 15-year-olds, 1970s toy-makers had to think afresh. Many innovative ideas grew out of technological advances. Children who had once been happy with jigsaws became hooked on breakthrough home-video games such as Pong, thanks to firms like Atari. The days of pull-along toys were numbered: youngsters cried out for battery-powered talking gizmos, like Dr Who's companion, K-9, by Palitoy. Stiff competition from inexpensive Far Eastern imports forced traditional diecast manufacturers like Corgi and Dinky to compromise on quality, resulting in higher proportions of moulded plastic pieces being introduced into models. But the increasing penetration of television in the home spawned a host of new toys, helping to keep classic makers afloat. Children's bedrooms soon filled up with a host of mementoes from screen favourites like *The Brady Bunch*, *Kojak*, *The Wombles* and *Wonder Woman*. But, just as parents were absorbed by the fitness craze, so were their children. Little legs were kept well exercised with the cult Chopper bicycle, and it was hard to separate 1970s kids from their skateboards.

↓ When Rolf Harris and his Young Generation dancers first spotlit the monophonic Stylophone on television's *The Rolf Harris Show*, little did they realize what impact this "pocket electronic organ" would have. Its inventor, Brian Jarvis, reputedly came up with the idea while repairing a toy piano for his niece. London-based Dubreq Ltd turned his electronic gem into a 1970s bestseller. Collectors, and there are plenty, nostalgically remember touching the metal "keyboard" with the pen-like "stylus" and listening to the stylophone "sing" on David Bowie's *Space Oddity*. A variety of models was produced – the white soprano was the girls' favourite. Look out for the rarer deluxe version, the 350S, with two styluses, presets and other advanced features.

Standard model (boxed) | £30–40 | $55–75

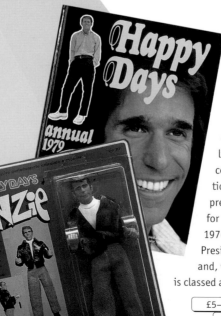

← The American comedy series *Happy Days* was the 1970s equivalent of *Friends*, with soda instead of *caffé latte*. Henry Winkler (b.1945) played the ultra-cool Fonz, the epitome of hip. When he got his library card there was a 500 per cent increase in library registrations in a month. The in-jokes and predictably happy stories lasted for 256 episodes; there was even a 1976 campaign to elect "Fonzie for President". Memorabilia abounds, and, with continual re-screenings, it is classed as cool to collect.

£5–6 | $9–11 | *Annual*
£30–40 | $55–75 | *Fonzie doll*

➜ Addicted players will never forget the race to assemble the Mouse Trap Game. It was another success from an American toy giant, the Ideal Toy Corporation (now part of Hasbro). With its peculiar array of plastic pieces that linked together to catch a toy mouse it offered the decade's youngsters hours of fun. Equally memorable is the Master Mind game launched by British-based Invicta Plastics Ltd in 1972. Billed as "A battle of wits and logic between two players", the idea could not have been simpler. The object was to break your opponent's code, which had been set by the choice of four coloured pegs. This is the 1973 version of the game, which is denoted by the addition of the "Game of the Year" award logo and the Design Centre triangle. Later editions are datable by other variants in the box design.

Mouse Trap	£5–10	$9–18
Master Mind	£3 6	$5 11

"Game of the year"

← *Dr Who*, the BBC television series first screened in 1963, went from strength to strength in the 1970s. New monsters, its début in colour and the arrival of two new Doctors, Jon Pertwee (1970) and Tom Baker (1974), kept children entertained. Baker's interpretation of the "Time Lord" helped the show to become a hit in the United States. He dressed more casually in an oversized coat, a wide-brimmed floppy hat and his trademark long multi-coloured scarf. He also had a new companion, the lovable pooch K-9. The British toy firm Palitoy wasted no time in marketing this impressive toy version of the Doctor's loyal robot dog, programmed with "lots of K-9 phrases".

£40–70	$75–125

→ Technological advances opened up a new world for 1970s youngsters – hand-held electronic games were no longer a thing of the future. MB, one of the leaders in the field, spawned a craze with its Simon game. The challenge was to keep up with the computer, following the random pattern of lights it selected at speed. Equally thrilling was the firm's Logic 5, a sequence-guessing game presented as truly up-to-the-minute with its Sinclair-style graphics and red LED display. Not to be left behind, Mattel, the manufacturers of Barbie, formed an electronics division to launch a run of compulsive games like this Football 2 from 1978.

Simon (boxed)	£30–35	$55–65
Logic 5	£5–10	$9–18
Football 2	£8–10	$15–18

"the challenge was to keep up with the computer"

← *The Magic Roundabout* was first shown on BBC television in 1965. Created by Serge Danot, it was based on a bunch of quirky characters, including Dougal the shaggy dog, Ermintrude the pink cow, Brian the snail and spring-loaded Zebedee. Its success was boosted from 1971 by licensed toys from Corgi. Boxed examples of this playground set, costing £6.30 in 1972, are now exceedingly rare. Dougal's money-box, issued in 1971, was a sure way of getting kids familiar with the new decimal currency.

Playground set	£500–1,500	$900–2,700
Money-box	£15–18	$25–30

← Billed as "the mightiest Ms on TV" and starring a former Miss America, Lynda Carter, Wonder Woman was the female equivalent of Superman. She started life as a cartoon character in 1942, created by a consultant to DC comics, William Moulton Marston. The television series starring Carter was first aired by ABC in 1976 as *The New Original Wonder Woman*. Needless to say, young girls soon mimicked her twirling ball of light transformation and hot-pants costume, and tried to recreate her glamorous look with junior make-up sets. The ultimate was to own a Wonder Woman doll like this one by Mego. Released in 1978, it was the firm's second attempt at creating a look-alike character doll, and is distinguished from later issues by the painted rather than fabric bustier. If the original box is in good condition, as here, it does add significantly to the value.

£85–140 | $150–250

→ Thames Television's *Magpie*, which ran from 1968 to 1980, rivalled the BBC's hugely successful *Blue Peter* in popularity. Broadcast twice a week, it quickly gathered a loyal following among youngsters who could not stop humming the programme's "One for sorrow, two for joy ..." theme tune. It blended travel, nature and science reports with craft spots. There was even a feature with a young, relatively unknown Austrian body-builder, Arnold Schwarzenegger! Collectables include the sought-after run of ten *Magpie* badges and the classic Christmas annuals – this is the second, from 1970.

£4–5 | $7–9

← "Tiny" the giraffe was a character from another favourite children's television show, *The Enchanted House*. Dinky Toys (taken over by Airfix in 1971) gained a name for TV tie-ins like this natty model of Tiny's Mini Moke, featuring an opening bonnet and a removable canopy. Youngsters could also have hours of fun with the packaging, and because many followed the instructions to "cut out Tiny's friends", complete boxed toys like this are treasured. The owner of this Basil Brush toy by Corgi also avoided temptation and never removed him from the box.

Tiny's Mini Moke £90–140 | $165–250
Basil Brush £175–200 | $315–360

← The Chopper bicycle is a 1970s icon and a hot collectable, particularly in pristine condition as here. Named after the American term for a helicopter, it gave kids the "street cred" and independence they yearned for. The first designer bike for youngsters, it kept its British manufacturers, Raleigh, in top position for five years after its launch in 1970. Advertising was compulsive: "Once there were ships. Then there were aircraft. Now there is the hovercraft ... and the wild new fun bike from Raleigh." The Chopper was more expensive than a standard child's bike, but its radical design introduced a new breed of pedal power worth paying for. This is a sought-after Mark 2 version, with sloping main tube and curved back tube, which appeared in 1971–72.

| £300–500 | $540–900 |

→ It took a lot of talent and imagination to bring a group of puppets to life. But, thanks to Jim Henson (1936–90), who had created puppets for *Sesame Street* from 1969, *The Muppet Show* was born in 1976. Hosted by the fast-talking Kermit the Frog, it introduced us to unforgettable characters like Miss Piggy, Fozzie Bear and Gonzo. Guest appearances from stars such as Twiggy, Vincent Price, Elton John and Rudolf Nureyev meant that adults and children alike were hooked. Henson collaborated with the British television company ATV, and this Muppet Show game by Palitoy carries the ATV logo. In 1979 Corgi produced the first of a series of Muppet Show models that are now catching collectors' eyes, as are other Muppet mementoes like this tambourine by Noble & Cooley.

| Tambourine | £15–18 | $25–30 |
| Game | £25–35 | $45–65 |

→ In 1975 the video-games giant Atari released a home version of its arcade game Pong. The graphics were basic and the idea was simple, but a new craze was born. In the comfort of their own homes, plugging into the family's television, kids pitted their wits against computers or friends. This "Video Sport Leisure Centre" from Grandstand Leisure offered "10 exciting games", from squash to soccer. As more collectors become interested in electronic games, consoles like this with all the accessories are increasingly prized.

£10–15	$18–25

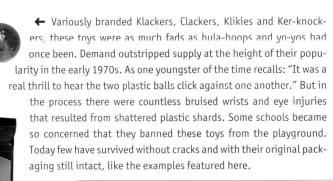

← Variously branded Klackers, Clackers, Klikies and Ker-knockers, these toys were as much fads as hula-hoops and yo-yos had once been. Demand outstripped supply at the height of their popularity in the early 1970s. As one youngster of the time recalls: "It was a real thrill to hear the two plastic balls click against one another." But in the process there were countless bruised wrists and eye injuries that resulted from shattered plastic shards. Some schools became so concerned that they banned these toys from the playground. Today few have survived without cracks and with their original packaging still intact, like the examples featured here.

£5–15	$9–25	Each

→ "Col Steve Austin, astronaut, a man barely alive. Gentlemen, we can rebuild him, we have the technology. We have the capability to make the world's first Bionic Man." So went the opening lines from the cult American television series *Six Million Dollar Man* (1974–78). The actor Lee Majors (b.1939) played the test pilot who, after crash-landing, was rebuilt into a superhero with bionic legs, arm and eye at a cost of six million dollars. The first Bionic Man dolls by Kenner appeared in 1975, and a stream of merchandising followed, including this 1978 lunchbox by Aladdin and this 1979 annual.

Annual	£3–4	$5–7
Lunchbox	£50–65	$90–120

← Keen to develop a television series packed with action but fitting with women's lib, Spelling/Goldberg Productions came up with *Charlie's Angels*. It was the number one show in its first season (1976–77), with over 23 million American households tuning in to watch. Probably more merchandising was linked to this show than to any other in the 1970s, including a Farrah Fawcett-branded shampoo. Although Farrah (b.1947), then married to Lee Majors, was only with *Charlie's Angels* for a year, plenty of mementoes, like this doll by Hasbro, mark her involvement as private investigator Jill Munroe.

| £55–70 | $95–125 |

→ This miniature golf set by the American firm Marx is a great reminder of how "the King of golf", Arnold Palmer (b.1929), first started. When he was just four years old his father presented him with his first set of specially cut-down clubs, and the rest is history. During his professional career Palmer won 92 championships, including the Masters four times, the US and Canadian Opens, and the British Open twice. His wins were widely televised at a time when sports coverage was booming. Not surprisingly youngsters wanted to own a set like this to copy one of golfing's greats. It promised, just like the thrill of the fairway, "all the elements of real golf".

| £20–30 | $35–55 |

← The American stunt rider Evel Knievel (b.1938) was the sort of "do-or-die" hero that 1970s kids worshipped. His death-defying motorbike jumps over lines of 50 cars, 13 double-decker buses and even a tank full of sharks became legendary. Half of all American households tuned in to watch his 1975 jump over 14 Greyhound buses. Predictably the international star spawned a host of toys such as this rare battery-powered Evel Knievel toothbrush, complete with a plastic jump ramp.

| £165–185 | $300–330 |

← Despite losing to Brazil in the 1970 World Cup, Britain was awash with football fever this decade. Palitoy, famed for introducing Britain's youngsters to Action Man in 1966, took advantage of the craze with a run of Sportsman figures from 1968 to 1973, including this fast-kicking footballer. Fans of specific clubs could mix and match their teams' strips, using the "Famous Football Club" range of outfits. This figure dates from 1970 when Action Man's much trumpeted spray-on "realistic hair" replaced his previously moulded locks. Swapping football stickers in the playground was a sure way to keep on top of the action, but few complete sticker books survive in good condition today.

Sticker album	£25–30	$37–45
Action Man	£100–250	$180–450

→ After reading that around 30 per cent of marriages in the United States brought together spouses who already had children, Sherwood Schwartz hit upon the idea for the television series *The Brady Bunch* (first aired 1969). It followed the clean-living lifestyle of the Brady newly-weds: mum Carol with her three daughters, and dad Mike with his three sons. This lunchbox from Thermos was a favourite for those struck by "Bradymania". Just as popular was merchandising from *The Partridge Family* series (1970–74), including an official magazine, Viewmaster cards, knitting patterns, items relating to heart-throb David Cassidy, and annuals like this.

Annual	£5–6	$9–11
Lunchbox	£175–225	$315–400

→ "We'd go for miles for a good slope with smooth tarmac," recalls one keen 1970s skateboarder. This was the golden age of skateboarding, and dedicated outdoor parks and specialist competitions took the sport to new heights. "Sidewalk surfing" boomed, thanks to the American Frank Nasworthy's new polyurethane wheels, called Cadillacs, coupled with the invention of press-in precision bearings. The decade's skateboarders had more control, could go faster and did not have to worry about going flying if they hit gravel. Classic 1970s boards by great names like Powell Peralta and Dogtown can be worth as much as £330, or $495, apiece. Roller-skating also had a new lease of life during the 1970s, and sports centres resounded to the beat of the roller disco.

Skateboard	£18–25	$30–45
Roller-skates	£10–12	$18–20

"Who loves ya, baby?"

← Lt Theo Kojak was one of television's most popular detectives. Telly Savalas (1924–94) played "the personality cop who gets the job done" in the long-running American series (from 1973) that was syndicated to Europe. Kojak was a sweet-talking ("Who loves ya, baby?"), fast-moving ("It's the fuzz baby, come on open up") guy, different from other 1970s cops, such as Columbo, because he had a bald head and sucked a lollipop. This detective game from Arrow Games Ltd was aimed at eight-year-olds who wanted to "Join the Kojak Squad". Corgi made this Kojak Buick diecast car, as well as this red Ford Torino from another popular 1970s television series, Starsky and Hutch.

£5–10	$9–18	Detective game
£70–80	$125–145	Kojak Buick
£70–80	$125–145	Ford Torino

→ The Wombles, created by the British author Elisabeth Beresford while she was out walking on Wimbledon Common, first appeared as characters in her 1968 book of the same name. But it was the five-minute slots on television, along with Mike Batt's chart-topping Womble songs, that brought these ultimate recyclers to life. Youngsters knew all the lyrics to *The Wombling Song* (the one that began "Underground, overground, wombling free, the Wombles of Wimbledon Common are we ...") and sang along to other pop tunes like *Remember You're a Womble*. This Pelham puppet of Madame Cholet, the Womble cook, was one of the best-made Womble toys. The seemingly endless range of memorabilia extended to Womble chocolate bars and Viewmaster slides, and also included Christmastime favourites such as the 1975 annual and this jigsaw puzzle.

Puppet (boxed)	£25–30	$45–55
Annual	£4–5	$7–9
Jigsaw	£4–5	$7–9

← With the advent of decimalization in the United Kingdom in 1971, money was firmly on the agenda. For children who needed to master the nation's new currency, what better way to do it than with a brand new money-box? These three were all made by the British pottery firm Carlton Ware, and were designed by its in-house stylist Vivienne Brennan. The flat-back shape seen here in the soldier and policeman boxes meant that they were easy to decorate with a range of lithographic transfers. Collectors can find these relatively frequently, but might struggle to secure one of the rarer "bug eye" money-boxes like the snail example featured here. Look out for the Carlton Ware mark on the base.

£25–45	$45–80	Flat backs (each)
£30–40	$55–75	Bug eye snail

117

rock and pop

There was an overriding sense of confusion in the music world as the 1970s dawned. The Beatles split up, and the last Isle of Wight festival in 1970 marked the end of the hippie era. Glam Rock soon took the place of folksy ballads, and fans had fresh looks to cultivate thanks to the outrageous outfits worn by rock greats like Elton John and the androgynous David Bowie. The Bee Gees proved instrumental in pushing the underground dance scene onto the international stage, and by the mid-1970s disco had arrived. Rebellious youngsters looking for a new kind of music embraced Punk, along with the rhythmic reggae lilt of Bob Marley and The Wailers, whose cry for unity influenced countless bands. Vintage vinyls make popular collectables, and true rarities can be worth large sums. Most, however, have little more than token value, unless they are unusual foreign pressings, have variant sleeves or were withdrawn. Even so it is worth keeping anything by cult 1970s bands because constant reassessments of the decade mean they are becoming increasingly sought after.

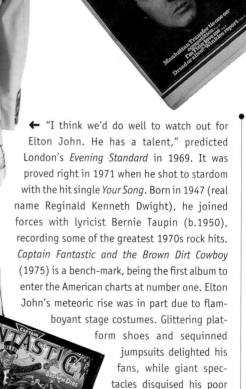

← "I think we'd do well to watch out for Elton John. He has a talent," predicted London's *Evening Standard* in 1969. It was proved right in 1971 when he shot to stardom with the hit single *Your Song*. Born in 1947 (real name Reginald Kenneth Dwight), he joined forces with lyricist Bernie Taupin (b.1950), recording some of the greatest 1970s rock hits. *Captain Fantastic and the Brown Dirt Cowboy* (1975) is a bench-mark, being the first album to enter the American charts at number one. Elton John's meteoric rise was in part due to flamboyant stage costumes. Glittering platform shoes and sequinned jumpsuits delighted his fans, while giant spectacles disguised his poor sight. This stage suit was custom-made for him by the tailor Bill Whitten. It is painted and embroidered with the cover illustration from the 1973 album *Goodbye Yellow Brick Road*.

£6–7	$11–13	Captain Fantastic album
£2,000–3,000	$3,600–5,400	Elton's stage suit

← The Beatles' split in 1970 shocked the music world, but in 1971 Paul McCartney (b.1942) formed Wings. The band had a string of number one singles, as well as chart-topping albums, before disbanding in 1981. Memorable successes included the theme for the 1972 Bond movie, *Live and Let Die*, and the number one Christmas single from 1977, *Mull of Kintyre*, which sold over 2.5 million copies; this accounts for its low value today. This poster, from the band's first American tour in 1976 when they played at the Cow Palace, San Francisco, is a coveted rarity. Wings' 1979 album, *Back to the Egg*, is often underrated, but this picture disc, intended for in-house use only, was an ultra-rare release from Parlophone Records.

"glittering platform shoes"

Back to the Egg promo picture disc	£1,200–1,500	$2,150–2,700
US tour poster	£170–180	$305–325
Record Mirror	£5–25	$9–45
Mull of Kintyre single	£1–3	$2–5

← After pointing at a random spot on a map of the United States (Bay City in Michigan), a tartan-clad Scottish group, the Bay City Rollers, was born. The group appeared on BBC television's *Top of The Pops* singing their first number one hit, *Bye Bye Baby*, in 1975. Rollermania swept Britain and soon spread across the Atlantic with their first American album, *Bay City Rollers*. *Wouldn't You Like It* (pictured at the back) was the band's third album (also from 1975). Fans could not get enough memorabilia, and these bubble-gum packs came complete with picture cards. It is rare to see them still boxed, just as they were sold. As many mothers discovered, the only way to make sure that their children helped in the kitchen was to buy a Bay City Rollers tea-towel as shown here.

£4–5	$7–9	Album
£100–125	$180–225	Bubble gum and picture cards
£5–8	$9–15	Tea-towel
£60–80	$110–145	Shoes

→ The Osmonds were a singing sensation who hit the big time internationally when young Donny and Marie joined their barbershop-singing brothers Alan, Wayne, Merrill, Jay and little Jimmy. *I'm Leaving It All Up To You* (1974), with 16-year-old Donny and 14-year-old Marie pictured on the cover, was the first of their joint albums. The Osmonds' success spawned the hugely popular *Donny and Marie Show* (1976–9), which included an unforgettable spot where Marie sang "A little bit of country", and Donny followed with "A little bit of rock and roll". Memorabilia ran from lunchboxes and annuals to sewing patterns like this, a result of Marie's link-up with Butterick in 1978.

Sewing pattern	£7–8	$13–15
1975 Osmonds annual	£2–3	$3–5
I'm Leaving It All Up To You album	£5–6	$9–11

← Performance was as much a part of rock at this time as the music itself. With his androgynous posturings, spangled jumpsuits and "girlie" eye make-up, David Bowie (b.1947, real name David Jones) embraced the essence of "Glam Rock". The cover of his 1973 album, *Aladdin Sane*, sparked head-lines of "Oh you pretty thing" in the music journal *Melody Maker*. The American rock band Kiss also turned to costume – thigh-high platform boots, leather codpieces and kabuki-style make-up – to present a dramatic alter ego. This is a French original of their *Dynasty* album (1979).

Aladdin Sane	£4–5	$7–9
Dynasty French original	£18–20	$30–35

→ Civil rights campaigners put the issue of black rights firmly on the agenda in the 1970s. Music and film became vehicles for social expression, and movies made by and for blacks commanded record audiences. Hollywood responded with a run of big-budget "blaxploitation" films with a new breed of hero, the "supercool" black crime buster. The most memorable was *Shaft* (1971), starring Richard Roundtree, with an Oscar-winning soundtrack by Isaac Hayes (b.1942) that sold millions of copies. It has recently been rediscovered by collectors, along with his soundtrack to *Tough Guys* (1974), as a result of the release of an updated *Shaft* movie in 2000. James Brown (b.1933) was called in to write the soundtrack for *Slaughter's Big Rip-off* (1973), another gem, led by his unforgettable soul track *People Get Up and Drive Your Funky Soul*.

Tough Guys	£20–25	$35–45
Slaughter's Big Rip-off	£55–60	$95–110
Shaft	£9–10	$16–18

← Pink Floyd was one of the most successful rock bands of the 1970s and beyond. From its underground beginnings and début at the launch of the radical newspaper *International Times* in 1966, the band (named after bluesmen Pink Anderson and Floyd Council) soon became idolized worldwide. Its psychedelic 1960s act gave way to what fans described as "ethereal numbers", which started to seep through on the album *Atom Heart Mother* (1970). With *Dark Side of the Moon* (1973) the group's instrumentals on songs like *Money* and *Time* cemented their iconic status. The London-based design company Hipgnosis (est.1968) worked on both of these album covers. This copy of *Dark Side of the Moon* differs from the 25 million sold to date because it is a rare tour edition in pink vinyl.

£140–150	$250–270	Dark Side of the Moon tour edition
£8–10	$15–18	Atom Heart Mother

← Led Zeppelin's fourth album, known simply as *IV* (1971), gave music a new direction with its unique blend of folk, blues and hard rock. Robert Plant's distinctive vocals coupled with guitarist Jimmy Page's technical skill delivered one of rock's most played songs, *Stairway to Heaven*. Millions of copies were sold, so its value is relatively low. Captain Beefheart (b.1941 as Don Glen Vliet) also fused musical genres. With his Magic Band he brought together rock, blues and free jazz in albums like *Captain Beefheart and the Spotlight Kid* (1972).

The Spotlight Kid	£14–15	$20–25
Led Zeppelin IV	£5–6	$9–11

→ On a hot Whitsun bank holiday in 1970 a crowd of over 400,000 converged on Afton Down on the Isle of Wight for "3 days of peace's music". It was the last flourishing of the hippie era. The official ticket price was £3, but by Sunday the festival was declared "free" as the corrugated fencing was torn down. "It was the best line-up ever assembled on a British stage," recalls one music fan: The Doors, The Who and Jimi Hendrix, who was dead just three weeks later. A representative from Apple Records used this backstage pass on 30 August 1970. Like the promotional poster it is emblazoned with David Roe's classic psychedelic drummer illustration.

Poster	£150–160	$270–290
Backstage pass	£60–70	$110–125

"3 days of peace's music"

← When Fleetwood Mac released the album *Rumours* in 1977 it seemed to echo liberated society's turmoils. Marriage splits, like those experienced by the band's members, became more commonplace in the 1970s, so the lyrics of songs like *Go Your Own Way* and *Dreams* were deeply meaningful for many. This is a poster for *Rumours*, which won the coveted Grammy Award for "Album of the Year". At the other end of the spectrum was the Grateful Dead, an American band which embodied the "magic" of drugs. This poster promotes the 1975 album, *Blues for Allah*, and features the same Phillip Garris artwork as the album cover.

£50–70	$90–125	*Fleetwood Mac poster*
£120–180	$215–325	*Grateful Dead poster*

→ When the British-born Bee Gees (an abbreviation of Brothers Gibb) were asked to record a soundtrack for a new movie called *Saturday Night Fever*, no one realized just what a hit it would be. With songs like the pulsating theme, *Stayin' Alive*, and *Night Fever*, the album sold in its millions and helped to make the dance craze international. Disco fans could not get enough of the brotherly trio (Barry, Maurice and Robin Gibb), whose bright white smiles, matching suits and soaringly high harmonies were mimicked at every turn. *Here at last...Bee Gees...Live* (1977) was the group's only official live album, which was recorded at a concert given in Los Angeles in December 1976. For youngsters smitten with the band's music there were countless mementoes, including jigsaw puzzles as illustrated here.

Saturday Night Fever	£6–8	$11–15
...Live album	£7–8	$13–15
Puzzle	£16–18	$25–30

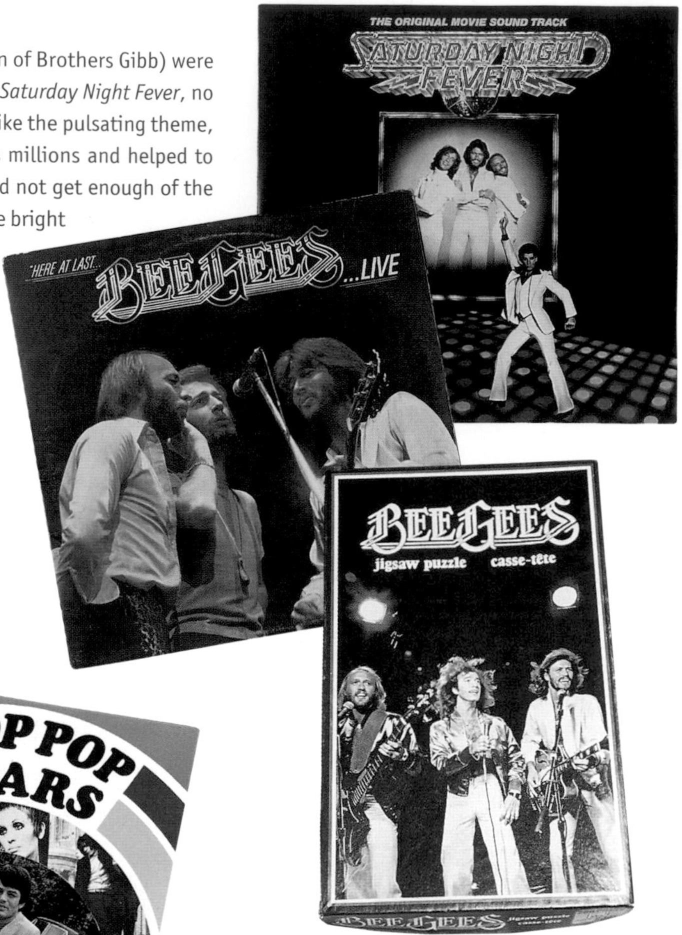

"Saturday Night Fever"

← Compilation albums were an inexpensive way of hearing the latest hits without buying the official band albums. Fans had to be careful as cut-price albums often featured re-recorded tracks, but *Disco Hits 75* (1975) proudly claimed to give "20 original hits" from artists like the Bay City Rollers, The Three Degrees and Gary Glitter. Arcade Records, like K-tel which also specialized in compilations, promoted its albums with well-placed television advertising. The *Top Pop Stars* series of annuals from the British publishers Parnell gave fans a behind-the-scenes look at their favourite bands. This edition from 1970 shows BBC Radio One's first disc jockey and *Top of the Pops* host, Tony Blackburn, on the front cover.

Top Pop Stars 1970	£5–8	$9–15
Disco Hits 1975	£4–5	$7–9

← The best-selling album *Breakfast in America* (1979) marked a change of direction for the British rock band Supertramp, formed in 1969. Tracks such as *Logical Song*, *Goodbye Stranger* and the album's title song had virtually permanent exposure on the radio. The cover of this album epitomizes the British fascination with American culture in the 1970s. As well as denim jeans, American situation comedies and movies, the fast-food giant McDonald's opened its first restaurant in London in 1974.

£3–4	$5–7

→ The 1974 Eurovision Song Contest was held in Brighton, England. The Swedish pop quartet Abba took to the stage to sing *Waterloo* and "Abbamania" was born. "They were sophisticated and everything we wanted to be," recalls one fan, who tried to replicate their glitzy on-stage style. Matchbox's now valuable dolls satisfied youngsters, while the *Arrival* album (1976) is classed as a masterpiece by fans. Its lead song, *Dancing Queen*, was their biggest hit and only American number one. A year on *Abba – The Album* was released, before their big-screen debut in *Abba – The Movie* (1978).

Abba dolls (set)	£800–900	$1,450–1,600
Abba – The Album	£2–3	$3–5
Waterloo picture disc (German version)	£45–50	$80–90

← Although he had already recorded an album and starred in the cult movie *The Rocky Horror Picture Show* (1975), it was with the album *Bat Out Of Hell* that the American singer Meat Loaf (b. 1946, real name Marvin Lee Aday) shot to superstardom in 1977. The combination of Jim Steinman's powerful songs and Meat Loaf's screaming vocals ensured that this was a chart-topper. This rare picture disc has the same Richard Corben illustration as the album cover.

£18–20	$27–30

→ The Boomtown Rats (formed in 1975 in Ireland) were the first new-wave band to appear on BBC television's *Top of the Pops*. Their music hit a chord with disaffected youngsters everywhere, ensuring that *Rat Trap* from their second album, *A Tonic for the Troops*, (released 1978 in Britain, 1979 in the United States) shot to number one in the British charts. *I Don't Like Mondays* (1979) saw the Rats go truly international, although many American radio stations banned it after Brenda Spencer from San Diego shot her classmates saying she didn't like Mondays. The British singer Kate Bush put a feminist spin on 1970s music. "Listeners know they are in the presence of a real woman who ... deals with life as it is being lived, not as it is supposed to be lived in the perfume ads," said *Stereo Review* in 1978 after the release of *The Kick Inside*. Watch out for the rare picture-disc version of this album.

A Tonic for the Troops	£2–3	$3–5
The Kick Inside (signed)	£20–25	$35–45
Signed Boomtown Rats photograph	£15–20	$25–35

"Sniffin' Glue ... And Other Rock 'n' Roll Habits"

← The aim of the First European Punk Festival, which was held in Arènes de Mont de Marsan in 1976, was to spotlight France as a leading force in the new-wave music movement. Needless to say, conflict saw The Sex Pistols thrown out of the event and The Clash withdraw in sympathy. News of Punk gatherings was spread through fanzines such as *Sniffin' Glue ... And Other Rock 'n' Roll Habits*, launched in July 1976 and edited by the lead singer of the British Punk band Alternative TV, Mark P(erry). This is issue 4, featuring articles on The Jam, The Clash and The Buzzcocks.

£20–30	$35–55	Sniffin' Glue
£250–350	$450–630	Punk Rock poster

→ The hypnotic rhythms and passionate lyrics that the reggae artist Bob Marley (1945–81) achieved with The Wailers grew out of Jamaican ska music, which carries a powerful message of unity. "The songs echo the wailings of the ghetto not only in Jamaica but indeed in any concrete jungle anywhere," said text promoting *Catch A Fire* (1973), shown here in its "Zippo" sleeve. The ska/reggae artist Ken Lazarus was a major influence on The Specials and Madness in the late 1970s.

Today's Pleasure	£8–10	$15–18
Catch A Fire	£40–60	$75–110

← Colour touched almost every aspect of life in the 1970s, from clothes to kitchens, so not surprisingly coloured vinyl records were all the rage. The trend already existed, but really took hold in the new-wave Punk sector. Coloured singles were often reserved for foreign-market pressings, and can be valuable today. Some records were issued in a variety of different colours. Squeeze's *Cool for Cats* (1979) came in a range of vibrant tones – pink, red (the rarest), pale pink (as seen here), clear red and black. Prices vary, depending on the quantity issued and the number that have survived. In the case of the most valuable be wary of poor-quality fakes with fuzzy images.

£2–45	$3–80	Each

→ The unpredictability of The Sex Pistols has led to some of the most valuable Punk collectables. Possibly fewer than 100 copies of their single *God Save the Queen* (1977) on the A&M label exist. Production was halted after the Pistols managed to get embroiled in another skirmish. A few months later Virgin released *God Save the Queen* with a different backing track, now worth a fraction of the original. This concert poster from the band's Norwegian tour is a rare survivor, as is the autographed ticket for the band's last British "gig" in 1977.

Signed ticket for last UK gig	£1,500–1,750	$2,700–3,000
Live in Trondheim poster	£250–350	$450–630
God Save the Queen A&M single	£2,500–3,500	$4,500–6,300

film

Hollywood countered the threat of television in the 1970s with high-grossing, mass-appeal blockbusters. The unforgettable *Jaws* in 1975, directed by the 27-year-old Steven Spielberg, topped box-office statistics until George Lucas's epic *Star Wars* hit the scene in 1977. Equally groundbreaking were "up-close-and-personal" movies like *Love Story* and *Annie Hall*, the social realism of *Taxi Driver*, and the cult "blaxploitation" films. A new breed of stars emerged as advertising put actors like Jack Nicholson and Clint Eastwood on a pedestal alongside directing greats like Francis Ford Coppola and Martin Scorsese. Hollywood gave these directors from film schools an opportunity to reflect real life, and their status soon overtook that of the studios. The film world was given another boost by the arrival of video recorders – after the release of the first films on videotape in 1977, there was no looking back.

← In 1977 *Annie Hall*, with its new slant on relationships, beat *Star Wars* to win the Oscar for best picture. Subtitles flashed the unspoken thoughts of Alvy Singer, the bespectacled Woody Allen (b.1935), and girlfriend Annie Hall, played by Diane Keaton (b.1946). The adaptation of Ken Kesey's novel *One Flew Over the Cuckoo's Nest* was similarly incisive and highly emotional. Jack Nicholson (b.1937) played a seemingly misdiagnosed inmate of a mental hospital fighting institutional authority. In 1975 the movie won five Oscars, along with widespread acclaim among society's disaffected.

| £65–80 | $120–145 | Annie Hall (US) |
| £250–350 | $450–630 | Cuckoo's Nest (US) |

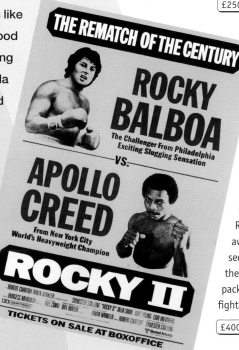

← After watching world champion heavyweight Muhammad Ali almost lose to the little-known Chuck Wepner in 1975, Sylvester Stallone (b.1946) penned the first *Rocky* story. The familiar plot of an underdog proving himself, this time in the boxing ring, took just three days to write and a mere month to film on a shoestring budget. Released in 1976, *Rocky* won a string of awards and shot Stallone to stardom. Four sequels resulted, and this poster promoted the second, *Rocky II*, released in 1979 and packed with the same exciting training and fight scenes as its predecessor.

| £400–500 | $720–900 | Rocky II (US) |

→ "It's you against the great white shark," said the sales line on this Jaws game. "One wrong move ... and the JAWS go snap!" Memories of the 1975 film *Jaws*, which catapulted its director, Steven Spielberg (b.1946), to Hollywood's A-list, were still very fresh when this child's toy appeared. The tale of a hungry shark that terrorized an Atlantic beach community was full of suspense, thanks to an ultra-realistic automated fish and John Williams's pulsating musical score. Peter Benchley, who wrote the original *Jaws* novel in 1971, delivered an equally thrilling script that kept movie-goers on the edge of their seats.

| £30–40 | $55–75 |

"One wrong move... and the JAWS go snap!"

← Bond still thrilled audiences, but in the 1970s British agent 007 was a new man. From 1973 and the release of *Live and Let Die*, the British actor Roger Moore (b.1927) played the suave spy. He was brought up-to-date with an LED dig-ital watch and an amphibious Lotus Esprit, which spawned a host of Corgi miniatures. Other collectables, such as this advance American poster for *The Man with the Golden Gun* (1974), are much sought after. *Moonraker* (1979), following hot on the heels of *Star Wars*, took Bond deep into space, as shown in this American poster illustrated by Dan Gouzee.

| £300–350 | $540–630 | *left*
| £200–250 | $360–450 | *right*

→ For those who saw *Star Wars: A New Hope, Episode IV* in 1977, the closing words of the old Jedi Knight, Obi-wan Kenobi, were unforgettable – "Remember, the Force will be with you, always." The huge box-office hit, written and directed by George Lucas (b.1944), took space adventure into a new ultra-realistic realm with fast action and fantastic special effects. It spawned a host of merchandising, from cereal packets to over 250 million 3¼in (8.5cm) plastic figures made by Kenner, part of the American toy giant Hasbro. Their fully moveable limbs revolutionized the toy-soldier world, and a reported five out of every six youngsters had a Star Wars memento, which even included soaps shaped as the quirky and adorable robot duo Artoo-Detoo and See-Threepio. A decade later these once hot treasures became car-boot-sale cast-offs. But boosted by the digital re-release of the original movies, plus the screening of *The Phantom Menace, Episode I* in the late 1990s, officially licensed vintage pieces are being fought over again – this time by nostalgic grown ups.

Star Wars poster (Australian)	£50–60	$75–90
Darth Vader (16½in/42cm)	£80–100	$120–150
Star Wars Pop-Up Book (UK First)	£17–23	$25–34
Soaps (each)	£18–20	$27–30

← The sense of realism that director Martin Scorsese (b.1942) injected into the 1976 film *Taxi Driver* broke new ground. The storyline follows a Vietnam veteran, Travis Bickle, played by Robert De Niro (b.1943), who takes a job as a New York cab driver to cure his insomnia. The violence on the streets turns Bickle into a self-appointed vigilante. Scorsese's portrayal of society's dark corners was a marked move away from what had gone before. This poster by Guy Peellaert is highly sought after. The classic racing-car movie *Le Mans*, released in 1971, linked real footage from the 1970 24-hour event with filmed sequences in which the lead actor Steve McQueen (1930–80) drove himself. The result was a new documentary style of film, packed with Porsches, frenetic racing and the inevitable slow-motion crashes.

Taxi Driver (US)	£250–400	$450–720
Le Mans (Japanese)	£265–465	$475–835

→ "A great tradition returns: The Gangster Movie" said the publicity for *Get Carter* (1970). With it came a fresh look for the British actor Michael Caine (b.1933), who dispensed with the endearing image seen in his 1960s movies *The Italian Job* and *Alfie* to play the hard-nosed, icy-cool, small-time killer Jack Carter. But the true masterpiece of this new genre had to be *The Godfather* (1972), directed by Francis Ford Coppola (b.1939) and based on Mario Puzo's best-selling novel from 1969. "A man who doesn't spend time with his family can never be a real man," pronounced its Oscar-winning star, Marlon Brando (b.1924), in the role of the Mafia family's patriarch, Don Vito Corleone.

Get Carter (Australian)	£130–200	$235–360
The Godfather (UK)	£250–400	$450–720

"This is a .44 Magnum – the most powerful hand gun in the world ... you've got to ask yourself one question, do I feel lucky. Well, do ya, punk?" Only the tough-talking San Franciscan detective Harry Callahan, played by Clint Eastwood (b.1930), could have said these words in what became one of the most memorable movie scenes of the decade. The film *Dirty Harry* (1971), so-called because Harry "always gets the shit end of the stick", presented a character whom the public identified with – one who wanted to get the job done without bureaucracy and red tape. During filming Eastwood met the poster designer Bill Gold and asked him to create a run of posters for *Dirty Harry* and its sequels, *Magnum Force* (1973) and *The Enforcer* (1977). For collectors such posters sum up the power of each film and stand alone as good pieces of 1970s artwork.

Dirty Harry (US advance)	£2,500–3,000	$4,500–5,400
Magnum Force (US)	£1,000–1,200	$1,800–2,150

→ You did not go to see a Bruce Lee movie for the storyline, you went to see it for the captivating fight sequences. *Enter the Dragon* (1973), the last film Lee (1940–73) completed before his death, was a benchmark, kick-starting the Kung Fu craze. Despite its being "X-rated" in the United Kingdom, viewable only by adults, youngsters were always trying to replicate the action. Martial-arts movies were becoming popular, but this was the first American-Hong Kong co-production. Lee was branded a true hero with the fast-moving, high-kicking action that he choreographed. Interest in this genre is growing, and posters like this are prized.

Enter the Dragon (UK)	£300–400	$540–720

← "Artistically despicable," reported *The Sunday Telegraph*, and "sickening and disgusting" added the moral campaigner Mary Whitehouse after the release of Stanley Kubrick's (1928–99) controversial movie *Clockwork Orange* in 1972. Despite being "X-rated" it still shocked a nation with graphic portrayals of sex and "ultraviolence". This promotional poster sums up the plot: "Being the adventures of a young man [Alex, played by Malcolm McDowell] whose principal interests are rape, ultra-violence and Beethoven." Press reports about supposed copy-cat crimes, the birth of a menacing "Clockwork cult" and studies of how the film affected viewers' hearts led Kubrick to ban it in the United Kingdom. Like Kubrick, the American director Francis Ford Coppola (b.1939) used violent scenes to convey a message powerfully in the epic film *Apocalypse Now* (1979) about the real horrors of the war in Vietnam.

Clockwork Orange programme	£30–35	$55–65
Clockwork Orange (UK)	£350–550	$630–1,000
Apocalypse Now (US)	£200–265	$360–475

→ "They call her Coffy and she'll cream you!" was the promotional line for this movie. In the run of "blaxploitation" films produced in the early 1970s, *Coffy* (1973) ranks high, pitching its heroine, Coffy, played by Pam Grier (b.1949), as a female version of Richard Roundtree's super-cool character *Shaft* (see p.120). The opening scene, where Grier blasts away a sleazy drug-pusher and then injects his assistant with a fatal heroin overdose, has all the elements of good black versus white evil. For poster collectors it is material from key films in the genre like *Coffy* that are the most desirable.

Coffy (US)	£135–165	$200–250

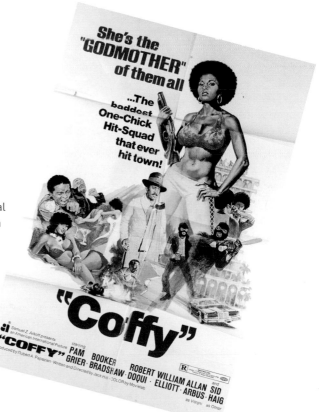

books

Fresh legislation advanced equality in both sex and race, and 1970s literature drew on these new-found freedoms for inspiration. The Australian author Germaine Greer upheld Women's Lib in *The Female Eunuch* (1970), hitting out against a male-dominated society. Equally challenging was Shirley Conran's domestic manifesto, *Superwoman*, which stressed: "Life is too short to stuff a mushroom." Real-life issues spilled over into fiction too. Alex Haley's *Roots* tackled African-American rights, while Richard Bach's seemingly easy-going tale of a young seagull was read by some as a cue for the disadvantaged to break free. Reflections on the counter-culture of the 1960s provided fodder for plenty of authors like Jim Carroll and Hunter S. Thompson, and, despite a noticeable softening of relations between the Superpowers, the Cold War remained a hook for the spy genre. Bestsellers included Stephen King's spine-chilling tales of horror and Douglas Adams's quirky take on galactic travel. Book collectors prize award-winning first editions, so look out for titles that won the highly coveted Booker, Pulitzer and Whitbread prizes. Clean first-edition copies without any tears or scribbles, complete with their original dustjackets, are worth considerably more than battered well-read equivalents.

→ *Gravity's Rainbow* (1973) is regarded as "arguably the most important literary text since [James Joyce's] *Ulysses*." Its reclusive writer, Thomas Pynchon (b.1937), reportedly handwrote the entire 700-page novel on graph paper. With this, his third book, he won countless honours including the National Book Award, which he declined, and the William Dean Howells Medal for the best work of fiction to appear in the United States over a five-year period. Signed copies of Pynchon's early novels are exceptionally rare and can be worth five-figure sums.

US First | £1,725–2,500 | $1,725–3,100

← With his first book, *Father Christmas* (pub.1973), the author and illustrator Raymond Briggs (b.1934) painted a comical picture of Santa dealing with everyday problems. His line of humanizing went even further when he created *Fungus the Bogeyman* (1977), which transformed a potentially scary monster into an adorable beast with unusual living habits. This example is a UK first edition. In the guise of a children's novel, *Watership Down* (1974) by the British author Richard Adams (b.1920) touched on real-life issues. It followed a family of rabbits in their quest for a new home far away from the threat of housing development. The meaningful tale won *The Guardian* award for children's fiction and the Library Association's Carnegie Medal. This is an Australian first edition.

Fungus the Bogeyman | £35–40 | $65–75
Watership Down (1972) | £85–100 | $155–180

➜ Hidden within much 1970s popular fiction were social messages. Richard Bach's *Jonathan Livingston Seagull* (1970) follows the story of a young seagull in his quest to break away from society's shackles and fly free. Alex Haley (1921–92) spent twelve years tracing his ancestors back to the days of slavery, when his great-great-great-great grandfather was alive, for his influential book *Roots* (1976), bringing African-American issues to the forefront. And in 1975 Malcolm Bradbury (1932–2000) used academic life as a politically charged backdrop for *The History Man*. Gender issues were raised when lecturer Howard Kirk preyed on his female students.

The History Man (UK First)	£70–75	$125–135
J.L. Seagull (US Deluxe First signed)	£150–160	$270–290
Roots (UK First)	£85–100	$155–180

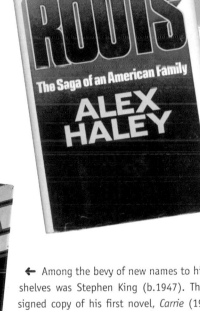

← Among the bevy of new names to hit our bookshelves was Stephen King (b.1947). This is a rare signed copy of his first novel, *Carrie* (1974), which firmly revived the horror genre. Today first editions of King's bestsellers are issued in their millions, but when *Carrie* was published the initial print run was far smaller – hence its collectability. *Riotous Assembly* (1971) launched the career of the novelist Tom Sharpe (b.1928), and with it came a new style of comic writing. When it was first sold, it cost readers just 38 shillings (£1.90) but today Sharpe's admirers value it far higher. Martin Amis (b.1949) was another writer who made his debut in the 1970s. Copies of his first book, *The Rachel Papers* (1973), which won a Somerset Maugham Award, are scarce.

Carrie (US First signed)	£770–850	$1,400–1,550
The Rachel Papers (UK First)	£300–400	$540–720
Riotous Assembly (US First)	£60–65	$110–120

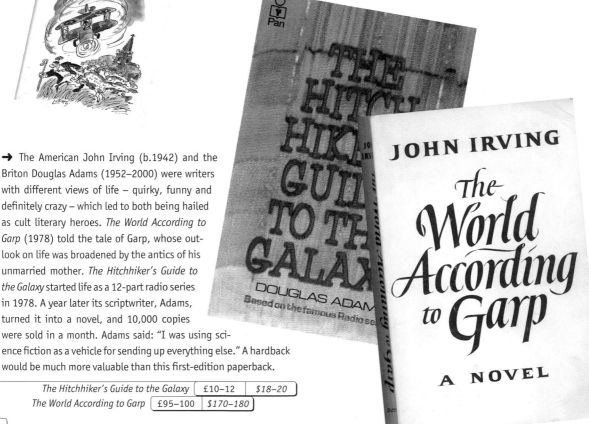

← The escapades of a vet in rural Yorkshire were an improbable subject for a string of bestsellers, but they struck gold for the British author James Alfred Wight (1916–95), whose pen name was James Herriot. Highly autobiographical books, their popularity was sealed thanks to a film of the first, *All Creatures Great and Small,* screened in 1974, and a BBC television series of the same name from 1978. Richard Patrick Russ (1914–2000), who changed his name to Patrick O'Brian, injected a renewed vigour into an unusual genre, the historical maritime novel. This is a rare British first edition of his first book, *Master and Commander*, published in 1970. O'Brian focused on the seafaring adventures of two characters, Lt Jack Aubrey and physician Stephen Maturin, throughout his 20-book epic.

£11–13	$20–25	*Vets Might Fly*
£11–13	$20–25	*Vet in a Spin*
£730–830	$1,300–1,500	*Master & Commander*

→ The American John Irving (b.1942) and the Briton Douglas Adams (1952–2000) were writers with different views of life – quirky, funny and definitely crazy – which led to both being hailed as cult literary heroes. *The World According to Garp* (1978) told the tale of Garp, whose outlook on life was broadened by the antics of his unmarried mother. *The Hitchhiker's Guide to the Galaxy* started life as a 12-part radio series in 1978. A year later its scriptwriter, Adams, turned it into a novel, and 10,000 copies were sold in a month. Adams said: "I was using science fiction as a vehicle for sending up everything else." A hardback would be much more valuable than this first-edition paperback.

The Hitchhiker's Guide to the Galaxy	£10–12	$18–20
The World According to Garp	£95–100	$170–180

"We were somewhere around Barstow on the edge of the desert when the drugs began to take hold ..." The influence of 1960s drug culture ran through into Hunter S. Thompson's (b.1939) *Fear and Loathing in Las Vegas* (1971). It is prized as much for its bizarre prose as for Ralph Steadman's hilarious ink drawings. A fellow American, Jim Carroll (b.1950), started writing *The Basketball Diaries* (1978) when he was 12 years old – with tales of stealing to support his heroin addiction which "are as much fiction as biography", according to his introductory note. This first edition, with a photograph of Carroll taken by Rosemary Klemfuss (later his wife) and silver lettering, is the most collectable.

| £535–565 | $960–1,000 | The Basketball Diaries (US first) |
| £1,700–1,800 | $3,000–3,250 | Fear and Loathing (signed US first) |

→ Relations between the United States and the Soviet Union were tense despite moves towards *détente* with the signing of Salt I and II (Strategic Arms Limitations Treaties) in 1972 and 1979. The Cold War harboured suspicion and fear, which the British writers John le Carré (b.1931) and Frederick Forsyth (b.1938) harnessed for their thrillers. This is a rare proof copy of *Tinker, Tailor, Soldier, Spy* (1974), classed as le Carré's masterpiece. The first in his acclaimed "Quest for Karla" trilogy, it features the British Secret Service agent George Smiley. Unlike Ian Fleming's fast-moving James Bond books, le Carré's fiction was cleverly paced. As the plot unfolded, so did a new genre of spy novel. Forsyth's *The Day of the Jackal* (1971) presented another believable account of espionage. Its central character, a hired British assassin codenamed "The Jackal", is involved in a daring plot to murder General Charles de Gaulle. The thriller was made into a film two years later.

| £400–600 | $720–1,100 | The Day of the Jackal (signed UK first) |
| £370–385 | $665–690 | Tinker, Tailor, Soldier, Spy (UK proof copy) |

useful addresses

where to buy

The following shops and antique dealers offer a range of collectables from the 1970s. Markets and fairs are also good hunting grounds.

dealers

Alfie's Antiques Market
13–25 Church Street
London NW8 8DT, UK
Tel. (0044) 020 7723 6066
Website: www.alfiesantiques.com
At Alfie's:
Antigo *Decorative Arts*
Biba Lives *Vintage Clothing*
 Tel. (0044) 020 7258 7999
 Website: www.bibalives.com
Paolo Bonino *Decorative Arts*
 Mobile 07767 498 766
Glassworks *Italian glass*
Francesca Martire *Jewellery and Packaging*
Tel. (0044) 020 7724 4802
The Girl Can't Help It
 American-themed fashions and household items
 Tel. (0044) 020 7724 8984
 Website: www.sparklemoore.com
Persiflage *Women's Fashions, Accessories, Lingerie and Swimwear*
 Tel. (0044) 020 7724 7366

Ballyhoo Vintage Clothing
230 North 2nd Street
Philapelphia
PA 19106, USA
Tel. (001) 215 627 1700
Website:
www.ballyhoovintage.com

Beanos
Middle Street
Croydon CR0 1RE, UK
Tel. (0044) 020 8680 1202
e-mail: shop@beanos.co.uk
Website: www.beanos.co.uk
Second-hand recorded music

Bookmark Children's Books
Fortnight
Wick Down, Broad Hinton
Swindon SN4 9NR, UK
Tel. (0044) 01793 731693

CenturyModern
2928 Main Street
Dallas 75226
Texas, USA
Tel. (001) 214 651 9200
Website: www.centurymodern.com
Modern furniture, design and accessories

Charles Jeffreys Posters & Graphics
4 Vardens Road
London SW11 1RH, UK
Tel. (0044) 020 7978 7976
Website: www.cjposters.com

Christina Bishop
Tel. (0044) 020 7221 4688
Fax: (0044) 020 7221 3989
Period kitchenware
(by appointment only)

Cooking the Books
The Glen
Saint Brides Netherwent
Caldicot NP26 3AT, UK
Tel. (0044) 01633 400150
Out-of-print cookery books

The Country Seat
Huntercombe Manor Barn
Nr Henley-on-Thames
Oxfordshire RG9 5RY, UK
Tel. (0044) 01491 641349
Website: www.thecountryseat.com
Post-war design and furniture

Crazy Clothes Connection
134 Lancaster Road
London W11 1QU, UK
Tel. (0044) 020 7221 3989
Clothing from the 1920s to the 1970s

deiltak.com
28 Gillespie Crescent
Edinburgh EH10 4HU, UK
Tel. (0044) 0131 228 6638
First editions worldwide

Denby China Matching
Tree Garth, Church End
Ravensden, Bedford MK44 2RP, UK
Tel. Bruce Edwards:
(0044) 01234 771745

Denby Pottery Visitor Centre
Derby Road, Denby
Derbyshire DE5 8NX, UK
Tel. (0044) 01773 740799

Design70
3 Rue Saint Francois de Paule
06300 Nice, France
Tel. (0033) 0 493 80 42 62
Website: www.design70.com
Design site

Didier Antiques
58–60 Kensington Church Street
London W8 4DB
Tel. (0044) 020 7938 2537
Designer jewellery
(by appointment only)

EtceteraDesign
Website: www.etceteradesign.com
Jan Ekselius reproduction furniture

Festival
136 South Ealing Road
London W5 4QJ, UK
Tel. (0044) 020 8840 9333
e-mail: festival51@btconnect.com
Midwinter and Portmeirion ceramics

Fiftie-Fiftie
Kloosterstraat 156, 2000 Antwerp
Belgium H.R.A. 314845
Tel. (0032) 3 237 43 72
Website: www.fiftie-fiftie.be
Modern design and furniture

First Call/Wardrobe
51 Upper North Street
Brighton BN1 3FH, UK
Tel. (0044) 01273 202201
Vintage clothing for sale or hire

Flying Duck Enterprises
320–322 Creek Road
Greenwich, London SE10 9SW, UK
Tel. (0044) 020 8858 1964
Household wares and decorative arts

Frasers Autographs
399 The Strand
London WC2R 0LX, UK
Tel. (0044) 020 7836 9325
www.fraserautographs.com

Freeforms Mid-Century Ceramics and Glass
Gallery 215
2nd Floor
The Showplace
40 West 25th Street
New York NY 10010, USA
Tel. (001) 845 300 8021
Website: www.freeformsusa.com
Glass and ceramics

Genie's Fab Fabrics
Stall 52, Snooper's Paradise
7/8 Kensington Gardens
Brighton BN1 4AL, UK
Website:
www.thebrighton.demon.co.uk
Period soft furnishings, curtains, and linen

Glitter & Dazzle
Pat and Ken Thompson
Tel. (0044) 01329 288678
Designer jewellery

Hardy's Collectables
862 Christchurch Road
Boscombe East
Pokesdown
Bournemouth
Dorset BH27 6DQ, UK
Tel. (0044) 01202 422407
20th-century collectables

JetsetModern
Broadway Antique Market
6130 N. Broadway
Chicago
IL 60660, USA
Tel. (001) 773 743 5444
Website: www.jetsetmodern.com
Modern design

Ken Lopez – Bookseller
51 Huntingdon Road
Hadley, MA 01035, USA
Tel. (001) 413 584 4827
Website: www.lopezbooks.com
Modern literary first editions

Modcity
Website: www.gomod.com
20th-century design and home furniture portal

The Modhaus
Website: www.modhaus.com
Tel. (001) 617 822 9183
Vintage furniture and decorative arts site with a showroom open by appointment

Nigel Wiggin
The Old Hall Club, Sandford House
Levedale, Stafford ST18 9AH, UK
Tel. (0044) 01785 780376
Website: www.oldhallclub.co.uk
Old Hall tableware

post
Unit H33, Camden Stables
Camden Market, Chalk Farm Road
London NW1 4AH, UK
Tel. (0044) 020 8341 4897
Mobile 07901 637608
Website: www.postdesign.co.uk
Post-war design – furniture, lighting, ceramics and glass

RetroFunk
2918 North FM 620 192
Austin, Texas 78734, USA
Tel. (001) 512 266 8935
e-mail: Hipster@Retrofunk.com
Website: Retrofunk.com
1970s collectables

Retrokit
Website: www.retrokit.co.uk
Site specializing in retro technology

RetroModern.com
805 Peachtree Street, Atlanta
GA 30308, USA
Tel. (001) 404 724 0093
Fax: (001) 404 724 0424
e-mail: mail@retromodern.com
Re-issues of post-war originals, with particular emphasis on design from the late 1960s through to the present

Sarah Potter
Tel. (0044) 020 7627 0570
*Post-war design
(by appointment only)*

The Reel Poster Gallery
72 Westbourne Grove
London W2 5SH, UK
Tel. (0044) 020 7727 4488
Website: www.reel-poster.com
Film posters

Alvin Ross Toys
Tel. (0044) 01865 772409
e-mail:
alvin@vintage-games.co.uk
Website:
www.vintage-games.co.uk

Helen Martin Carlton Ware
Website: www.carltonware.biz
Tel. (0044) 01636 611 171
Mobile 07774 147 197
e-mail: helen@carltonware.biz
Leading Carlton Ware Specialist

Target Gallery
7 Windmill Street
London W1P 1HF, UK
Tel. (0044) 020 7636 6295
Modern Design

Timewarp Toys and Collectables
P.O. Box 632
Phoenicia
NY 12464, USA
Tel. (001) 845 688 2221
Website: www.timewarptoys.com
Vintage toys and collectables

20th Century Marks
"Whitegates"
Rectory Road
Little Burstead
Near Billericay
Essex CM12 9TR, UK
Tel. (0044) 01268 411 000
Website:
www.20thcenturymarks.co.uk
Classic post-war design

Twenty Twenty One
274 Upper Street
London N1 2UA, UK
Tel. (0044) 020 7288 1996
Website:
www.twentytwentyone.com
Furniture, design and decorative arts

Ulysses
40 Museum Street
London WC1A 1LT, UK
Tel. (0044) 020 7831 1600
Fax: (0044) 020 7419 0070
e-mail: ulyssesbooks@FSBDial.co.uk
Modern literary first editions

Whitford Fine Art
St James's
London SW1Y 6BN, UK
Tel. (0044) 0207 930 9332
Website:
www.whitfordfineart.com
Decorative arts

Wiseman Originals Ltd
34 West Square
London SE11 4SP, UK
Tel. (0044) 020 7587 0747
Fax: (0044) 020 7793 8817
Website:
www.wisemanoriginals.com
Modern prints

XXO
78 Rue de la Fraternité
93230 Romainville, France
Tel. (0033) 1 48 18 08 88
Website: www.xxo.com
1970s furniture and design

Yorkshire Relics of Haworth
11 Main Street, Haworth
West Yorkshire BD22 8DE, UK
Tel. (0044) 01535 642218
Classic records and television-related books

auction houses

Bonhams, New Bond St
101 New Bond Street
London W1S 1SR
Tel. (0044) 0207 629 6602
Website: www.bonhams.com

Bonhams, Knightsbridge
Montpelier Street
London SW7 1HH, UK
Tel. (0044) 020 7393 3900
Fax: (0044) 020 7393 3905
Website: www.bonhams.com

Bonhams & Butterfields
USA
Tel. (001) 415 861 7500
www.butterfields.com

Christie's
8 King Street, St James's
London SW1 6QT, UK
Tel. (0044) 020 7839 9060
Fax: (0044) 020 7839 1611
Website: www.christies.com

Christie's South Kensington
85 Old Brompton Road
London SW7 3LD, UK
Tel. (0044) 020 7581 7611
Website: www.christies.com

Christie's New York
20 Rockefeller Plaza
New York, NY 10020, USA
Tel: (001) 212 636 2000
Website: www.christies.com

Christie's Los Angeles
360 North Camden Drive
Beverley Hills, CA 90210, USA
Tel. (001) 310 385 2600
Website: www.christies.com

Los Angeles Modern Auctions
P.O. Box 462006, Los Angeles
CA 9046, USA
Tel. (001) 323 845 9456
Website: www.lamodern.com

Saffron Walden Saleroom
1 Market Street
Saffron Walden
Essex CB10 1JB, UK
Tel. (0044) 01799 513281

Skinner
The Heritage on the Garden
63 Park Plaza, Boston
MA 02116, USA
Tel. (001) 617 350 5400
Fax: (001) 617 350 5429
Website: www.skinnerinc.com

Sotheby's London
34–35 New Bond Street
London SW1A 2AA, UK
Tel. (0044) 020 7293 5000
Fax: (0044) 020 7293 5989
Website: www.sothebys.com
Sotheby's no longer have a dedicated collectables department, but do deal with independent experts

Sotheby's New York
1334 York Avenue at 72nd Street
New York, NY 10021, USA
Tel. (001) 212 606 7000
Fax: (001) 212 606 7107
Website: www.sothebys.com

bibliography

books

Ambasz, Emilio, *Italy: the new domestic landscape* (exhibition catalogue), Museum of Modern Art, New York 1972

Austen, Diana and Davies, Catherine, *Good Housekeeping Kitchens,* Ebury Press 1976

Branzi, Andrea, *The hot house: Italian new wave design,* Thames & Hudson 1984

Carter, Alison, *Underwear: the fashion history,* Batsford 1992

de la Haye, Amy, *The cutting edge: 50 years of British fashion 1947–1997,* V&A Publications 1997

Decelle, Philippe, *L'utopie du tout plastique, 1960–1973,* Editions Normand 1994

Fiell, Charlotte and Peter, *Modern Chairs,* Taschen 1993

Fiell, Charlotte and Peter, *1000 chairs,* Taschen 1997

Fiell, Charlotte and Peter, *70s Decorative Art,* Taschen 2000

Garner, Philippe, *Twentieth Century Furniture,* Phaidon 1980

Garner, Philippe, *Contemporary Decorative Arts from 1940 to the present day,* Apple Press 1980

Gilmour, Sarah, *The 70s: punks, glam rockers & new romantics,* Heinemann 1999

Hall, Alan, *Action Man: the ultimate collector's guide,* Middleton Press 1999

Hardyment, Christina, *Slice of Life,* BBC Books 1995

Harris, Carol, *Miller's Collecting Fashion & Accessories,* Miller's 2000

Herald, Jacqueline, *The 1970s,* Batsford 1992

Higgins, *Katherine, Are You Rich?,* André Deutsch 2000

Hopwood, Irene and Gordon, *Denby Pottery 1809–1997,* Richard Dennis 1997

Jenkins, Steven, *Midwinter Pottery,* Richard Dennis 1997

Jenkins, Steven and McKay, Stephen P., *Portmeirion Pottery,* Richard Dennis 2000

Kaiser, Niels-Jorgen, *Verner Panton,* Bording Grafik 1986

Katz, Sylvia, *Classic Plastics,* Thames & Hudson 1984

Knowles, Eric, *Miller's Collecting Royal Memorabilia,* Miller's 1994

Leath, Peter, *The Designs of Kathie Winkle,* Richard Dennis 1999

Newman, Karoline, *A Century of Style: Lingerie,* Apple Press 1998

Opie, Robert, *Remember When,* Mitchell Beazley 1999

Polhemus, Ted, *Street Style,* Thames & Hudson 1994

Ponti, Gio, *Domus,* Editoriale Domus 1970/71

Porter, Catherine, *Miller's Collecting Books,* Miller's 1995

Powell, Aubrey, *Classic Album Covers of the 70s,* Dragon's World 1994

Radice, Barbara, *Ettore Sottsass: a critical biography,* Thames & Hudson 1993

Raimondi, Giuseppe, *Italian living design: three decades of interiors,* Tauris Parke 1990

Raimondi, Giuseppe, *Three Decades of Interior Decoration 1960–1990,* Rizzoli 1990

Sambonet, Guia, *Alchimia, 1977–1987,* Allemandi 1986

Sparke, Penny, *Furniture, Twentieth Century Design,* Bell & Hyman 1986

Sparke, Penny, *Electrical Appliances, Twentieth Century Design,* Bell & Hyman 1987

Sparke, Penny, *A Century of Design,* Mitchell Beazley 1998

Sparke, Penny, *Italian Design: 1870 to the Present,* Thames & Hudson 1998

Sparke, Penny, *Ettore Sottsass Jnr,* Design Council 1982

Design since 1945 (exhibition catalogue), Philadelphia Museum of Art 1983

magazines

Decorative Art in Modern Interiors, Studio Vista 1970–78
Ideal Home, 1970–79
Homes & Gardens, 1970–79
Nova, selected 1970s issues
Vogue, 1970–79

websites

www.baseballhalloffame.org
www.mrshowbiz.go.com
www.amazon.com
www.craftscouncil.org.uk
www.bieffeplast.com
www.louis-poulsen.com
www.corning.com
www.knoll.com
www.oluce.com
www.computerhistory.org
www.mos.org
www.watchspace.org
www.scandinaviandesign.com
www.iittala.fi
www.worldcuparchive.com
www.worldsony.com
www.toynutz.com
www.geocities.com
www.about.com
www.tv.cream.org
www.historychannel.com
www.biography.com
www.nvg.ntnu.no/sinclair/planet
www.classic-tv.com

index

ACKNOWLEDGMENTS

special thanks to...

Simon Andrew, Simon Alderson, Sarah Allen, Abigail Baker, Debbie Bee (*Nova* Magazine), Christina Bishop, Paolo Bonino, Margaret Bonner, Caroline Butler, Mike Chapman, Kathleen Curtis, Crazy Clothes Connection, Sue & Bruce Edwards, Anne & Leonora Excell, Ronda Fersky, Rhonda Fisher, Saffron Garner, Diane German, George Glastris, Maria Gibbs, Elizabeth Harris (Isle of Wight Glass), Jenny & Lawrence Hay, Pauline Hickton, Pat Higgins, John Hunter, David Huxtable, Michael Jeffery, Nick Jenkins, Steven Jenkins, John Jervis, David Lashmar, Matthew Line (*Homes & Gardens* Magazine), Lucia Lindsay, Ken Lopez, Hugo Marsh, Helen & Keith Martin, Adrian Mibus, Vibeke Mogensen (Louis Poulsen Lighting), Nigel Mynheer, Carolyn Oldershaw, Tina Oldknow (Corning Museum of Glass), Robert Opie, Clive Parks/Kathrin Van-Spyk/Shuna Harwood (First Call), Alexander Payne, Alan Peters, Albert Pfeiffer (Knoll Museum), Michael Pritchard, Anna Prince (Revlon), Jill Potterton, Mervyn Reese, Simon Robinson, Linda Salt, Anna Sanderson, Eddie Sandham, Trish Seal, Nina Sharman, Suzette Shields, Carolyn Shrosbee, Freya Simms, Emma Strouts, Karen Stylianides (*Ideal Home* Magazine), Steve Tanner & Lucile Guilbert, Pepe & Andrea Tozzo, Velma Wakeling, Magnus Wide, Caroline Wiseman, Nigel Wiggin, Philippa Windsor.

acknowledgments

MILLER'S COLLECTING THE 1970S

F cover btm ctr SK, F cover top ctr OPG/ST/PT, F cover top r CI, F cover btm l CI, F cover btm r OPG/ST/SJ, B cover top SPL, B cover btm RD(©AD)/BO, F flap BO, B flap top OPG/ST/FDE, B flap btm OPG/ST/KH, 1 KMM, 2 OPG/IB/SCA, 3 BO, 8–9 OPG/IB, 10 btm l OPG/ST/FDE, 10 btm r OPG/ST/DH, 11 btm l OPG/ST/KH, 11 btm ctr OPG/ST/DH, 11 btm r MP/RPG, 12 top l OPG/ST/PT, 12 btm ctr CI, 12 btm r OPG/ST/DH, 13 btm l OPG/ST/PT, 13 btm r OPG/ST/PT, 14 CP/P.Minsart, 16 top SPL, 16 btm l BO, 16–17 btm BO, 17 top r BO, 17 btm r CI, 18 top CI, 18 btm P, 19 top P, 19 ctr CI, 19 btm l CI, 20 top l SPL, 20 ctr r CI, 20 btm l SPL, 21 top l CI, 21 btm r CI, 22 top CI, 22 btm l VITRA, 23 top MK, 23 btm SPL, 24 ctr l OPG/ST/WFA, 24 btm CI, 24–25 top CI, 25 btm SPL, 26 top CI, 26 btm P, 27 top SK, 27 btm LAMA, 28 top l LAMA, 28 top r LAMA, 28–29 btm CI, 29 top l BAL/PC, 29 ctr r CI, 30 top ART, 30 btm l CI, 31 top r CC/© Fred Baier, 31 ctr l BO, 31 btm r CI, 32 top P, 32 btm OPG/ST/WFA, 33 top CI, 33 ctr P, 33 btm r BO, 34 top l LAMA, 34 btm CI, 35 top l CI, b ctr r CI, 35 btm l CI, 36 top l CI, 36 top r P, 36 btm l RD(©AD)/BO, 37 top r CI, 37 btm l OPG/ST/Z, 37 btm r OPG/ST/Z, 38 top l P, 38 ctr r MK, 38 btm l SPL, 39 top CI, 39 btm CI, 40 l CI, 40 btm r BO, 41 top l OPG/ST/Z, 41 ctr r OPG/ST/SP, 41 btm l CI, 42 top CI, 42 ctr l RO, 42 btm r CI, 43 top BO, 43 btm r OPG/ST/PBA, 44 top ctr r OPG/ST/PT, 44 ctr l OPG/ST/PT, 44 btm OPG/ST/DH, 75 top ctr l OPG/ST/PT, 45 top l P, 45 ctr OPG/ST/NJ, 45 btm OPG/ST/PT, 46 top r OPG/ST/KH, 46 ctr l SL, 46 btm l CSK, 47 top l OPG/ST/NJ, 47 top ctr BO, 47 top r OPG/ST/PT, 47 ctr l AWP/PC, 47 btm l RD/FDE, 48 top r SONY, 48 btm BO, 49 top l OPG/ST/NJ, 49 ctr l SPL, 49 btm r ET, 50 top KH, 50 btm OPG/ST/KH, 51 top l OPG/ST/KH, 51 ctr r OPG/ST/FDE, 51 btm l OPG/ST/PH, 51 btm ctr l OPG/ST/KH, 52 top l OPG/ST/CB, 52 ctr r OPG/ST/CB, 52 btm l OPG/ST/CB, 53 top r RD(©AD)/BO, 53 ctr l OPG/ST/CB, 53 ctr r OPG/ST/CB, 53 btm l RD(©AD)/PC, 54 l MP/MLC, 54 btm KMM, 55 top SPL, 55 ctr OPG/ST/SJ, 55 btm r OPG/ST/SJ, 56 top l OPG/ST/SJ, 56 btm ctr OPG/ST/SJ, 56 top r OPG/ST/SJ, 56 ctr l RD(©AD)/TG, 56 btm r OPG/ST/SJ, 57 top l DPC, 57 top r OPG/ST/SJ, 57 ctr r OPG/ST/SJ, 57 btm r OPG/ST/SJ, 58 top l OPG/IB/SCA, 58 ctr l OPG/IB/SCA, 58 btm WM, 59 top l OPG/IB/SCA, 59 top r OPG/IB/SCA, 59 btm l OPG/IB/SCA, 59 btm r OPG/IB/SCA, 60 top l P, 60 btm r OPG/ST/NJ, 61 top CI, 61 ctr l OPG/ST/SJ, 61 ctr OPG/ST/SJ, 61 btm r OPG/ST/KH, 62 top CSK, 62 btm OPG/IB/SCA, 63 top r BO, 63 ctr WM, 63 btm r CI, 64 top r OPG/ST/NJ, 64 btm l CI, 65 top SPL, 65 ctr KH/P, 65 btm OPG/ST/NJ, 66 top OPG/ST/KH, 66 ctr l OPG/ST/NJ, 66 btm OPG/ST/NJ, 67 top OPG/ST/NJ, 67 btm r OPG/ST/NJ, 68 top SPL, 68 btm CSK, 69 top OPG/ST/KH, 69 btm P, 70 top l P/©ADAGP, Paris and DACS, London 2001 (Victor Vasarely – poster "composition c.1970"), 70 btm © Sir Terry Frost "Colour On The Side of Blue", acrylic on canvas, 1971 from Wiseman Originals Ltd, 71 top l OPG/ST, 71 btm MP/PB, 72 top OPG/ST/DH, 72 btm l RF, 72 btm ctr RF, 73 top ctr OPG/ST/KH, 73 top r CI, 73 ctr l OPG/ST/DH, 73 btm l OPG/ST/DH, 73 btm ctr OPG/ST/DH, 74 top l RD/Hope & Glory, 74 top ctr OPG/ST/DH, 74 ctr l OPG/IB/SCA, 74 ctr OPG/ST/DH, 74 btm l OPG/ST/DH, 74 btm r OPG/ST/KH, 75 top ctr OPG/ST/KH, 75 top ctr r OPG/ST/KH, 75 ctr l OPG/ST/BO, 75 ctr ctr l OPG/ST/BO, 75 btm ctr OPG/ST/KH, 75 btm r OPG/ST/DH, 75 btm r OPG/ST/KH, 76 ©Henry Diltz/CORBIS, 78 top CSK, 78 btm l CSK, 79 r CSK, 80 top SNY, 80 top ctr l CSK, 80 btm l CSK, 80–81 ctr SNY, 81 top l OPG/ST/W, 81 top ctr PG/ST/W, 81 btm r CSK, 82 top l OPG/ST/W, 82 btm ctr OPG/ST/W, 82 btm r OPG/ST/W, 83 top l CSK, 83 top ctr OPG/ST/Z, 83 btm r CSK, 84 OPG/ST/CCC, 85 top r OPG/ST/W, 85 ctr l OPG/ST/W, 85 btm r OPG/ST/W, 86 top r OPG/ST/W, 86 ctr l OPG/ST/KH, 86 btm r CI, 87 top ctr OPG/ST/W, 87 top r OPG/ST/W, 87 btm OPG/ST/KH, 88 top r MP/F, 88 btm l CSK, 89 top l CSK, 89 ctr l CSK, 89 btm r CSK, 90 l SNY, 90 top r OPG/ST/KH, 91 top l CSK, 91 top r OPG/ST/W, 91 ctr ctr r OPG/ST/KH, 91 ctr r OPG/ST/C, 91 ctr top r OPG/ST/C, 91 btm r OPG/ST/KH, 91 btm r OPG/ST/W, 92 top CSK, 92 ctr OPG/ST/W, 92 btm OPG/ST/W, 93 top ctr l RO, 93 top r SNY, 93 ctr l OPG/ST/PBA, 93 btm RO, 94 top l OPG/ST/W, 94 top ctr l OPG/ST/W, 94 top ctr OPG/ST/CCC, 94 ctr CSK, 94 btm r RO, 95 top l RO, 95 top ctr l OPG/ST/CP, 95 ctr l RO, 95 ctr r CSK, 95 btm l RO, 95 btm ctr RO, 96 top RO, 96 btm RO, 96 btm r OPG/ST/DH, 97 ctr r RO, 97 ctr btm l OPG/ST/DH, 97 top l OPG/T/JMU, 97 btm l OPG/ST/DH, 98 top MP/G&D, 98 btm MP/DA, 99 top l CI, 99 ctr r OPG/ST/KH, 99 btm l CI, 100 top l OPG/ST/W, 100 top r OPG/ST/W, 100 btm OPG/ST/W, 101 top OPG/ST/W, 101 btm l OPG/ST/W, 101 btm r OPG/ST/W, 102 top l OPG/ST/W, 102 top r OPG/ST/KH, 102 btm ctr l OPG/ST/W, 102 btm r OPG/ST/W, 103 top l OPG/ST/W, 103 top r OPG/ST/W, 103 btm l OPG/ST/W, 103 btm ctr OPG/ST/W, 103 btm r OPG/ST/W, 104 top l OPG/ST/CCC, 104 ctr r OPG/ST/W, 104 ctr r OPG/ST/W, 104 btm l OPG/ST/W, 105 top l OPG/ST/W, 105 top r OPG/ST/W, 105 btm ctr l OPG/ST/W, 105 btm ctr r OPG/ST/KH, 106 © Roger Ressmeyer/CORBIS, 108 top OPG/ST/PT, 108 ctr btm RO, 108 ctr OPG/ST/FDE, 109 top ctr r OPG/ST/KH, 109 top r OPG/ST/BE, 110 ctr l OPG/ST/SJ, 110 ctr r OPG/ST/PT, 110 btm OPG/ST/DH, 110 btm ctr l BO, 111 top l RO, 111 ctr r OPG/ST/KH, 111 btm l CI, 111 btm ctr l CI, 112 top RD(©AD)/BO, 112 ctr r OPG/ST/DH, 112 btm ctr MP, 113 top ctr l RO, 113 top r OPG/ST/KH, 113 ctr ctr l OPG/ST/PH, 113 btm ctr r OPG/ST/FDE, 113 btm r SK, 114 top l RO, 114 top r RO, 114 btm l RO, 115 top l RD/BO, 115 top r SL, 115 btm r OPG/ST/KH, 115 btm ctr SK, 116 top r RO, 116 ctr r RO, 116 btm l CI, 116 btm ctr l RD/FDE, 117 top ctr r MP/HC, 117 top r MP/AR, 117 ctr ctr r RD/FDE, 117 ctr btm l SCA, 117 btm l OPG/IB/SCA, 118 l SPL, 118 top ctr l OPG/ST/BE, 118 top ctr r OPG/ST/JJ, 118 top r OPG/ST/BO, 118 btm r OPG/ST/BE, 119 ctr l MP/YRH, 119 ctr top OPG/ST/BE, 119 ctr btm RO, 119 btm ctr l OPG/T/JMU, 119 btm ctr r OPG/ST/FDE, 119 btm r OPG/ST/BE, 120 top l OPG/ST/BE, 120 ctr r OPG/ST/BE, 120 btm l OPG/ST/BE, 120 btm r OPG/ST/BO, 121 top l OPG/ST/BE, 121 top ctr OPG/ST/BE, 121 ctr ctr r OPG/ST/BE, 121 ctr r RO, 121 ctr r OPG/ST/BO, 121 btm l OPG/ST/BO, 122 top ctr l OPG/ST/BE, 122 top ctr r OPG/T/JMU, 122 top r OPG/ST/PT, 122 ctr l MP/20thCM, 122 btm l OPG/ST/PT, 123 top l OPG/ST/BE, 123 ctr top RO, 123 ctr btm OPG/ST/BE, 123 btm l OPG/ST/BE, 123 btm ctr r OPG/ST/BE, 124 top l MP/SW, 124 ctr top OPG/ST/BO, 124 btm l OPG/ST/BO, 124 btm r OPG/ST/BE, 125 l OPG/ST/PT, 125 top r OPG/ST/BE, 125 ctr btm OPG/ST/BO, 125 btm ctr l MP/F, 125 btm r OPG/ST/BE, 126 top l CI, 126 top r MP/RPG, 126 btm CI, 127 top l RO, 127 btm l CI, 127 btm ctr l CI, 128 top l OPG/ST/BO, 128 top r RO, 128 ctr r OPG/ST/JJ, 128 btm r OPG/ST/DH, 129 top l CI, 129 ctr l CI, 129 ctr r CI, 129 btm ctr CI, 130 top ctr CI, 130 ctr l CI, 130 btm r CI, 131 top l MP/SW, 131 ctr top l CI, 131 ctr btm l CI, 131 btm r CI, 132 top r 2000 KL, 132 ctr OPG/ST/KH, 132 btm 2000 KL, 133 top l OPG/ST/KH, 133 top r 2000 KL, 133 ctr l 2000 KL, 133 ctr ctr l OPG/KA, 133 ctr r 2000 KL, 133 btm 2000 KL, 134 top l D.COM, 134 top ctr 2000 KL, 134 ctr l D.COM, 134 ctr r D.COM, 134 btm r 2000 KL, 135 top l 2000 KL, 135 top ctr 2000 KL, 135 ctr btm OPG/KA, 135 btm r 2000 KL.

2000 KL – *2000 Ken Lopez – Bookseller*
20thCM – *20th Century Marks*
AR – *Alvin Ross*
ART – *Artifort Lande Ltd.*
AWP – *Andy Woods Photography*
B – *Beanos*
BAL – *Bridgeman Art Library*
BO – *Bonhams*
C – *Cenci*
© AD – *copyright André Deutsch*
CB – *Christina Bishop*
CC – *Crafts Council*
CCC – *Crazy Clothes Connection*
CI – *Christie's Images*
CP – *Camera Press*
CP – *Clive Parks*
CSK – *Christie's South Kensington*
D.COM – *deiltak.com*
DA – *Didier Antiques*

DH – *David Huxtable*
DPC – *The Denby Pottery Company*
ET – *Enrico Tedeschi*
F – *Frasers*
FDE – *Flying Duck Enterprises*
G&D – *Glitter & Dazzle*
HC – *Hardy's Collectables*
IB – *Ian Booth*
JJ – *John Jervis*
JMU – *Joyce Marie Umhey*
KA – *Ken Adlard*
KH – *Katherine Higgins*
KMM – *Keramik-Museum Mettlach*
LAMA – *Los Angeles Modern Arts*
MK – *Museo Kartell*
MLC – *Malcolm Law Collectables*
MP – *Miller's Publications*
NJ – *Nick Jenkins*
OPG – *Octopus Publishing Group Ltd*

P – *Phillips, London*
PB – *Phillips, Bath*
PBA – *Paolo Bonino at Alfie's Antiques Market*
PC – *Private Collection*
PH – *Pauline Hickton*
PT – *Pepe Tozzo*
RD – *R. Dixon*
REX – *Rex Features*
RF – *Ronda Fersky*
RO – *Robert Opie*
RPG – *Reel Poster Gallery*
SCA – *St Clere Antiques*
SJ – *Steven Jenkins*
SK – *Skinner, Auctioneers and Appraisers of Antiques and Fine Art, Boston, MA*
SL – *Sotheby's London*
SNY – *Sotheby's New York*
SONY – *Sony United Kingdom Limited*
SP – *Sarah Potter*

SPL – *Sotheby's Picture Library*
ST – *Steve Tanner*
SW – *Saffron Walden Saleroom*
T – *Timewarp*
TG – *Target Gallery*
VITRA – *Vitra Design Museum*
W – *Wardrobe*
WFA – *Whitford Fine Art*
WM – *Trustees of The Wedgwood Museum, Barlaston, Staffordshire*
YRH – *Yorkshire Relics of Haworth*
Z – *Zoom*

F – *Front*
B – *Back*
ctr – *centre*
r – *right*
l – *left*
btm – *bottom*